TIME FOR TRUTH

Other Books by Princess Ashraf Pahlavi

FACES IN A MIRROR

TIME
FOR TRUTH

by

PRINCESS ASHRAF PAHLAVI

IN PRINT PUBLISHING

Cover design and illustration by Lightbourne Images © 1995.

Front cover photo: Amidst sweeping enthusiasm of officers and recruits, Princess Ashraf Pahlavi visits a distant army post in the Iranian desert.

Back cover photo: On a lonely beach on the Persian Gulf Princess Ashraf Pahlavi and her son Shahriar.

Typesetting by AV Communications.

Publisher's Cataloging in Publication

Ashraf, Princess of Iran, 1919–
    Time for Truth / Ashraf Pahlavi.
    p. cm.
    Includes bibliographical references and index.
    Preassigned LCCN: 95-76051.
    ISBN: 1-886966-00-1.

1. Iran—History—Mohammed Reza Pahlavi, 1941–1979. 2. Iran—History—Revolution, 1979– 3. Iran—History—1979– 4. Iran—Politics and government—1941–1979. 5. Iran—Politics and government—1979– 6. Iran Hostage Crisis, 1979-1981. I. Title.

DS318.A74 1995   955'.05'3
                                  QBI95-229

Manufactured in the United States of America by Griffin Printing

CONTENTS

DEDICATION

I dedicate this book to the memory of my son
Shahriar and all Iranian men and women who
died for the freedom of the motherland.

PREFACE

O Phoenix, grant me the Resolve
On the road I take,
For the way is long
And I am a new wayfarer.

—Hafez

Today the Soviet Union no longer exists, a new Russia is born striving for democracy. But in neighboring Iran, we are not as fortunate. Like a comet of ill omen, the totalitarian tyranny imposed by Khomeini and his mullahs is about to enter the second millennium together with its long trail of evils. Ever since the great turmoil that shook Iran to its foundation in 1979, I have secretly kept a journal where, in addition to my own thoughts, I collected notes from books, documents, countless speeches and articles—with the hope of some day piecing together the truth behind the complicated events of the so-called Islamic Revolution. I knew this was a difficult task, for the unfolding of these events in Iran was not at all as it seemed to be and as it was reported in the media. Despite relationships of many years standing, Iran's history is far too intricate and far too unknown in the western world. I myself have often been baffled by the complexities of this puzzle, even though, in my case, I know where to look for answers. **On one issue I had**

no reservation whatever. From the beginning I had no doubts as to the nature and intent of the "mullarchy" which has devastated my country and worked relentlessly to erase all traces of Iranian civilization, indeed Iran's very identity.

I have never stopped speaking out against this alien and retrograde regime. When they tried to drown my voice, I bought space in newspapers, aired my thoughts and published numerous appeals. But for many years my voice has been a "cry in the wilderness." The United States which clearly helped Khomeini, did so by cloaking the old man in an aura of piety and sanctity—with the expectation that he would repay their efforts with conciliation, cooperation and, of course a tractable attitude on such crucial issues as oil and the security of the Persian Gulf region. Even now, after perceiving the grave mistake it made, the United States remains reluctant to fully acknowledge the nature of the Iranian Islamic regime, its worldwide terrorist networks, its dedication to the export of revolution, its goal to destabilize the entire Middle East and wreck the Arab peace process with Israel. Today, Tehran brands America "The Great Satan" and Washington counters by saying Iran is a "Rogue State." But a keen look at the billions of dollars of business between them, conveys an entirely different picture.

It is with this in mind that I feel compelled to reveal the material I have gathered. When I began writing this book America was riding high on the emotional roller coaster of the Iranian hostage crisis. As the exiled twin sister of the Shah of Iran, there were few takers for my views or those of the few officials of our regime who dared to speak out. Publishing this book in the circumstances that prevailed in the beginning of eighties, would have been considered at best ill-timed or at worst an interference in foreign policy. Indeed, the material assembled in this book forms a clear picture of an upheaval which could not have taken place without the assistance of our closest ally, the United States of America.

I have read many accounts on the Islamic revolution written by scholars, analysts, trained observers, or those directly involved in the drama. Many of them find it convenient to criticize my brother's policy of accelerated modernization. A design, which they say, was initiated by an authoritarian regime lacking in "safety valves." Modernization, they judged, disrupted the equilibrium of our society and generated a violent reaction of the masses who were deeply committed to religious tradition.

Individual writers single out particular aspects of this theme—the massive buildup of armaments and sophisticated industry, for example; the shortage of trained Iranian technicians which necessitated a large and visible foreign presence especially American. This, it is said, gave the Islamic right wing the "proof" they needed to convince their followers of the need to overthrow the Shah before western values would totally "corrupt" them.

I have seen other references to the authoritarian nature of the regime, to the "brutal" character of its U.S. trained police, as well as to the inequities in the distribution of wealth, the growth of large personal fortunes during the oil boom.

Others cite the blind confidence of members of the American Embassy in the regime. They suggest that diplomats, as well as agents of the CIA, who were out of touch with the currents of opposition, sent reports that "anesthetized" the White House and were themselves caught off balance by the oncoming crisis. Still others blame the indecisiveness of President Carter and the inconsistency of his aides who vacillated on courses of action, either picking the wrong alternative or the right alternative too late.

With all these explanations, the conclusion has always been the same: The problem lay with the Shah's policies and the blindness or inadequacies of the White House and its envoys to Iran. Yet factual though these observations may be, they do not go far enough: They raise as many questions as they seem to answer. I have struggled and wrestled with these questions again and again—sometimes even throughout the night—**Indeed it is "Time For Truth."** I am hopeful that in the pages of my journal, reality will show itself and be known.

If it *was* modernization as it is often claimed, which led to the fall of my brother's government, how can we explain the survival of institutions created by Ataturk in neighboring

Turkey, which for two centuries had been the seat of the Caliphate, its Sultan the Commander of the Faithful? Neither my father who greatly admired the Turkish leader, or my brother, who followed the same course with his "White Revolution," pushed secularization to the extent of government. Authoritarianism, for which he was and is still criticized, was not the exception in our part of the world. In fact, my brother's government was significantly less "absolute" than all those of our neighbors. I found the following statement in a book by Sir Anthony Parsons, Britain's ambassador to Iran between 1974 and 1980:

"As I got to know more Iranians intimately, I realized that Iran was not a police state in the absolute and all pervasive sense that we associate with European totalitarianism. In private, and in particular with foreigners, educated Iranians were persistently and devastatingly critical, not of the Shah's aims, but of ineffectiveness of the authorities to achieve them. These criticisms were voiced, so far as I could judge, more or less irrespective of who might be listening. This freedom of speech was some safety valve to compensate for the absence of democratic institutions. Another was the freedom to travel abroad and to export money." *(The Pride and the Fall. London 1984)*.

As for the CIA, I surely cannot believe what is being said about its inability to recognize and identify the opposition. Many sources, including the documents seized by "students" in the American Embassy, show clearly that the CIA was in regular contact with individuals who later became leaders of the new regime, that in fact attempts were even made to recruit Bani-Sadr who later became first President of Iran. In fact, American diplomats were so secure in their beliefs that they failed to destroy their Embassy's secret documents. Many Iranians, friendly to the U.S., were executed or had to flee the country because of this inexcusable laxness.

I think clearest when I am alone and when I can consider varying viewpoints. It is then that I often realize that mistakes were made. All my life I have been exceptionally close to my brother; and sometimes, I must admit, I did not recognize the full implications of what our government was doing. Yet our mistakes alone cannot explain the destruction of a 2500 year old monarchy, or the accession to power of a bloodthirsty mullarchy. My brother lost his throne to a powerful coalition of the Iranian Left and the Iranian Right, through calculated intervention of both our enemies and our friends. The motives of our enemies were clear, but those of our friends were not so clear and I believe, stemmed from failures of foreign policy on the highest level.

It now seems perfectly clear to me that our friends, Iran's allies, made grave and serious miscalculations, out of profound ignorance and misunderstanding of the oriental mind, of the tradition and nature of Iranian politics. It was this ignorance, as well as the cultural gap between east and west (the tendency of the west to judge others according to its own frame of reference) which made possible the systematic erosion of the regime through a campaign of unprecedented magnitude in the western media. The "army" which waged this campaign was often motivated by liberal values—values which have no exact counterpart in him. My brother who had been educated in Switzerland once told me: "Had the Iranians possessed the same mind set as Swedes, Swiss or French, I would have been the first to welcome and embrace full democracy on the spot."

I have long thought that the western mind, as well as the western media is all too anxious to judge and condemn a regime, which is, by their standards, not sufficiently democratic or liberal. In the case of our regime, this "anti" feeling was fed by opposition forces which, once in power, were in no way prepared to conform with western notions of "good government" or, for that matter, to repay western support with friendship. I could easily trace the motivations and goals of our traditional opponents, for these have a running thread through my country's long history. But I have had a more difficult time detailing the motivations of the United States, our principal ally for so many years.

It seems possible now to examine, somewhat more dispassionately, the various forces that cost my brother his throne and the Iranian people its freedom and prosperity. I believe it is also possible now for the west to re-examine with greater objectivity, my brother's value as an ally to the west and as a caring friend to the community of nations. The time has come also to re-evaluate the reasons why he was deemed dispensable, not only as an ally, but also as the legitimate ruler of the country. There are some sobering lessons to be gained from that period of our joint history and from the years that followed. The time has come to fathom the miscalculations made by those who orchestrated the removal of the Shah. It is crucial and urgent to examine the nature of this "Islamic Republic," and the great danger that the west has unleashed by providing extremists with power seat in the volatile and strategic area that surrounds Iran.

Sixteen years of bloody despotism have led my country to the brink of disaster, to a condition reminiscent of the turn of the century, when my father came out of the ranks to pull together the pieces of our nation. Today the picture is even far more disheartening: The efforts of generations of Iranians have been reduced to ashes by one of the most backward, despotic and ruthless regime on earth. Once upon a time, there, were more than 180,000 Iranians students in a single year, gladly studying in America, Europe or elsewhere abroad. The present regimes does not trust those who have studied in foreign lands... Following my brother's departure, more than two millions Iranians, including many highly educated men and women went into exile. Statistics show that in 1992, there were more Iranian doctors in Canada than Iran. As knowledge and education are considered dangerous, the Islamic regime has allowed a tragic brain drain to take place.

One of my brother's policies had been family planning. In 1994, a World Population Conference convened in Cairo. What the mullahs forgot to say there, was that they had devastated the national network created during the 1960s and 1970s and multiplied the birth rate. The net result has been the fastest rate of population growth in the world. From 36 million inhabitants in 1979 the population has jumped to 65 million. Presently, less than a third of school-age children are receiving an education and seven per cent of those desiring higher schooling can enter a university. A good half of our workforce is either unemployed or engaged in ephemeral occupations. The value of our currency has fallen to an all-time low. Inflation and prices are skyrocketing. From a lender nation and world wide aid donor with more than $30 billion in reserves abroad we have become a country in debt to the tune of $36 billion! The economy is crippled and operates at only one-third of its capacity. The press is totally muzzled by censorship. The population is highly disillusioned and restless. Riots are spreading, and there are great shortages everywhere. In 1992 there were countless crippled war veterans, more than 200,000 war widows and some 300,000 war orphans in Iran. Many teenage prisoners who returned from the awful war with Iraq are now embittered adults, with no work. Many are swallowed in criminal networks and have become addicted to drugs. The rate of suicide among our youths is one of the highest in the world.

Indeed, the decade that followed my brother's departure was one of untold sufferings for Iran. During that period more than a million Iranians were killed in urban guerilla operations, by firing squads, in prison under torture and, above all during the war with Iraq. This means that every hour of rule by the mullahs has cost the lives of at least ten of my compatriots. Amnesty International reports that daily arbitrary arrests, secret trials and summary executions are continuing. This is, in brief, the balance sheet of Khomeini's Islamic Republic.

For me, all that I hold dear is lost: My country, my brother, my younger son, navy captain Shahriar, cowardly assassinated by Khomeini's hired terrorists on a Paris street. I have no tears left to cry. In exile, I am a solitary spectator to the daily tragedies that ravage Iran and drain the lifeblood of our future generations. I still remember pictures of shoeless children, strips of red cloth tied around their heads, plastic keys to Allah's paradise hanging from their necks, pictures of Khomeini pinned to their chests—marching in close ranks across mine fields. I recall the explanations provided by an officer of the Ayatollah's holy war: "We do not have enough tanks and must economize our armored carriers." Chilling logic, to be sure, but perfectly consistent with the policies of a dictator who devalued human life to worthlessness. "Islam loves and honors its martyrs," said the old man from Qum, as he exhorted the masses in the execution of his grandiose schemes. But Khomeini did not love the people he ruled, he did not care for them, nor do the present leaders of the Islamic Republic. They only have utter contempt for Iran's past and all its centuries of civilization. Their aim is not the prosperity of the Iranian people but to brainwash and export terrorism. How did we fall in the hands of such a regime? Japanese Hara Kiri was not part of our tradition. Then perhaps we must start at the beginning and look at those who stood the greatest chance of becoming the principal beneficiaries of a crippled and decimated Iran.

1: THE INTERNATIONAL CAMPAIGN TO UNDERMINE IRAN

THE POWER OF THE MEDIA: After reading the latest news from Iran, I turn to a crossword puzzle for relief. I pause at the word "tyrant"—and when I turn to the answer, the word "shah" is given as a synonym. Years ago, I would have thrown the puzzle down in frustration and anger. Now I stare at the page, fascinated and, at the same time, repelled. This image, of my brother as a "tyrant," persists even now, when his worst enemies acknowledge that there is no common measure between his monarchy and the present reign of the mullahs. I recall reading a statement made by Rajavi, head of the Mujahiddin, after he escaped from Iran and arrived in Paris. "Khomeini is worse than Hitler, and the Shah was nothing but a choir boy."[1]

How did it begin, this well-orchestrated and relentless campaign to undermine my brother in the world press, to paint him as a ruthless and repressive tyrant? Whose interests were served? In *Spike*, a novel by Arnaud De Borchgrave and Robert Moss (New York, Avon, 1981), I read a fictional scenario which might well have been borrowed from life. A high-ranking Soviet defector testifies at a U.S. Senate hearing, describing tactics employed by the KGB Directorate: "We succeeded in depicting the Shah as a uniquely bloodthirsty tyrant, when in fact, his regime was mild compared with some of those in neighboring countries. Since our campaign to undermine the Shah was conducted so effectively through the western media, there was no need for us to attack him directly. On the contrary, we succeeded in maintaining the image of cordial relations until his overthrow was certain." When asked for specific examples, the defector cited a fabricated voice tape "of the Shah plotting counterrevolution with his generals that was faked under my personal instruction." To the question of how the tape was disseminated through American networks, he replied: "it wasn't difficult. We passed it via the Tudeh (Communist) Party in East Berlin, to Iranian students in Texas. They gave it to a local station, claiming it had come from a SAVAK defector. The denials and disclaimers are of no importance. It's the initial shock that shapes people's minds, not what's said afterwards." In De Borchgrave's novel, the tape in question was a three-day sensation in the United States. By the time voice experts had pronounced it a fraud, the "initial shock" had indeed been felt.

Last year a high-ranking Soviet official in the Russian Embassy in Tehran defected to the West. According to reports we have had from the intelligence community, the Russian has told a similar story, of anti-Shah material provided by the Soviets, channeled to the U.S., through the Iranian opposition in East Germany. I believe this was the way in which a fabricated voice tape of the Shah, calling on the military to stage a coup, was passed to Mike Wallace. (At the time, my brother was in Morocco.) Wallace called the royal palace there to verify the tape's authenticity. One of the Shah's aides told him the tape was not authentic, but Wallace aired it anyway. Although Wallace has since reconsidered his views on the Shah, he does not mention this incident in his book, *Close Encounters*.

I have an enormous file of many similar instances—articles and statistics which appeared in leading publications—demonstrating the power of systematic misinformation: In 1976, members of the American literary establishment invited to the United States Reza Baraheni, a professor of English and occasional poet. He was a dissident, pardoned by my brother, reinstated in his university position and allowed to travel freely abroad. With American assistance he published a collection of essays titled "The Crowned Cannibals," which contained such passages as: "The scale of torment was staggering. At least half a million people have once in their lifetime been beaten, whipped or tortured by SAVAK. In every household there is at least one person who was interrogated by SAVAK." These figures were never challenged. I am not a mathematician, but I know that the population of Iran is 37 million. If we estimate that each household consists of six persons, then, according to Baraheni's figures, SAVAK should have interrogated more than six million!

Today I have seen an old issue of *Time* magazine. It is dated August 16, 1976 and reports on a study of torture throughout the world. Concerning Iran, *Time* says: "Estimates of the number of political prisoners range from 25 to 100 thousand. It is widely believed that most of them have been tortured by the SAVAK, which secret police, French Lawyer Jean Michel Braunschweig (who investigated conditions in Iran last January), claims has 20,000 members and a network of 180,000 paid informers." If these figures were correct, it would have taken the SAVAK agents, if they worked seven days a week and 24 hours a day, half a century to perform interrogations and tortures on six million people (SAVAK was created in the early sixties)! It is curious that *Time* published this estimate of political prisoners rather than reproducing the estimate given by Amnesty International that same year: "It is impossible to assess with any accuracy the number of political prisoners in Iran, but there are certainly no fewer than 3,000."[2]

I recently found an article from the *Iran Times*,[3] in which Massud Rajavi, chief of the Mujahiddin, states: "The prisons of the Shah contained not more than 5000 persons (including ordinary criminals)."

Another particularly effective instance of misinformation concerns what is now known as "The Black Friday" or the "Jaleh Square Riots." On Friday, September 8, 1978, demonstrations in Jaleh Square, near the Parliament building, denigrated into riots. The government reported 58 dead and 205 wounded. The

AP reported that others died later, bringing the figure to 100. The UP quoted a figure of 95. Witnesses at the scene estimated the casualties at between two and three hundred. Members of the opposition, in their calls to foreign journalists, claimed 3,000 dead. Russ Braley, an American journalist who was in Tehran at the time, later observed: "The speed and the unanimity of the reports suggested that the figure was an organizational one, perhaps agreed on before the riot."[4]

A few days after the riot, the students advance a new casualty figure: 3,900. After Khomeini's return to Iran, Jaleh Square is renamed "Martyrs' Square" in order to "honor the 4,000 dead," a figure *Der Spiegel* publishes without reservation.

A few months later, the Islamic regime announces, through its foreign ministry, that 60,000 people have been killed during the revolution. Once elected President Bani Sadr adds some 5,000 to the figure. And when my brother flies from the Bahamas to Mexico City, the Khomeini embassy there charges that 365,995 people had been killed during the revolution. I have seen this kind of escalation time and time again.

Braley observes in a university lecture from which a report was printed on how such statistics are born. "About two months after the Jaleh Square, I visited National Front (an opposition group) headquarters in Tehran for a long talk with half a dozen of the leaders there. I was assured that the figure of 4,000 was correct. One of the Front leaders, a physician, told me: 'Why, only yesterday the Army killed 200 in the Bazaar.' I told him the town was full of reporters, not all of them in the pay of the Shah, and surely someone would have confirmed such a slaughter. He replied: 'Well, if not 200 were killed, then 200 were wounded.' In fact there had been shooting in the bazaar, and two persons were seen to drop, either hit or hitting the dirt. There was a lot of firing in the air at that period ... On February 12, 1979, almost a month after the Shah left, Iranian television reported 400 killed in Tehran that day alone, and there were clashes all over the country as the revolution's guns came out of hiding. My attempt to check figures leaves me not too far from the Shah's estimate of less than 1,000 killed in the revolution while he was in Iran."

I have often wondered why so many journalists and intellectuals accepted without reservation and without sufficient investigation, a picture of the Shah's regime which, though flawed, did not resemble the image circulated in the media. These people accepted the notion of a peaceful and benign Islamic government, a buttress against communist expansion, without understanding the nature of what was being unleashed on Iran and indeed on the entire Middle East. Now, with the evidence of six years before us, many have retrenched, reconsidered. Unfortunately, these sober second looks rarely have the impact of the "initial shock." For example, the London based Arab magazine, *Al Tadamun*, recently interviewed Rajavi, who said that in five years, Khomeini had executed 40,000, while "the Shah, against whom we revolted executed only a few hundred persons" (in a 38 year reign)...[5]

I still remember very well a Mike Wallace "Sixty Minutes" program in February 1980. On network television, and with an audience of millions, he painted a bleak picture of the Shah's regime and his secret police, citing cases of torture and accusing my brother and the CIA. Among the charges, he cited the Rex Cinema fire in Abadan (on August 29, 1978, arsonists poured gasoline in the exits of the Rex Theater, and 477 people burned to death). The clergy and the students claimed that SAVAK had set the fire in order to discredit the mullahs by attributing the blaze to them. Wallace went so far as to name the culprit (without checking) as an escaped police official "who is now living under an assumed name in Fresno, California." A few months later, in Tehran, a Muslim fanatic confessed to the crime, telling the judge that he had acted in the interests of the clergy: "It was oil that I was pouring on the fire of the revolution to hasten its success." Khomeini pardoned the arsonist and enrolled him in Hezbollah, the Party of God, whose only purpose is to suppress the enemies of the Islamic regime.[6] Wallace never mentioned this to his audience. Yet some four years later, in his book *Close Encounters*, he has this to say at the end of the chapter on Iran: "By the summer of 1982, there were no less than three wars raging in the Middle East; in Afghanistan, along the

Iranian-Iraqi border and in Lebanon, where Israeli troops were on the march. *It is possible that two of those wars, and perhaps all three, would never have broken out, had Anwar Sadat and the Shah of Iran been alive and in command of their respective governments.* (Italics mine). But by that time, both were in their graves, and, largely because of their demise, the future of the Middle East appeared to be more troubled and uncertain than ever before."

Recently I came across an interview in *The New York Times*[7] with Andre Laurens, director of *Le Monde*. In discussing the shrinking circulation of *Le Monde*, he made a statement which describes a problem which has become rather universal. "What we lost then (after the paper's glowing reports on Cambodia's Pol Pot and on Khomeini's Iran) was our elevation, our distance, and this hurt us. We were rather blind in foreign affairs, just not very lucid. But that's the story of the whole French intelligentsia." I could not, if I tried, overstate how powerful the effect was of this kind of week after week reporting on the "tyranny" of the Shah, and of his disregard for human rights. What happened in Iran is a striking example of how, in today's world, reality has become so susceptible to manipulation.

I recently read this observation by journalist-historian George Urban: "(The U.S.) didn't lose (the war in Vietnam) on the battlefields, but in Manhattan and the district of Columbia, through the special pleading and one-sided presentations of American television journalism."[8] In my brother's case, the loading of facts virtually dismissed the real achievements of his reign and made them all but nonexistent. Now even critics of our regime recognize these achievements. This is what Professor Marvin Zonis of the University of Chicago has written: "Some have argued that the changes which Iran witnessed in the 1970s were primarily cosmetic. That conclusion can result only from befuddled observations or muddled thinking. In fact, the changes were extensive and pervasive. An Iranian enemy of the Shah went into self-imposed exile from Iran in 1966. He returned to Iran after the Shah's departure in 1979 and spent several weeks traveling the countryside which he had not seen in 13 years. A professionally trained economist, he reported to me how he was staggered by the extent to which the economy, communications structures and social patterns of Tehran, to be sure, but also even the remote and formerly poverty-stricken villages had been transformed. Industrialization, collectivization, electrification, mechanization—with other concomitant processes had produced an Iran nearly unrecognizable to his trained eye."[9]

AMNESTY INTERNATIONAL: The role that this London based human rights organization played in the destabilization of Iran was a powerful one. Although conspiracy theories are unfashionable today among the intelligentsia, I feel I must write down what I know, that I must examine and raise questions about the activities of this group during the critical year of 1976. I had gotten hold of an internal circular issued by AI[10] in August of that year to all its national sections and coordinating groups. It preceded the publication of a briefing paper on Iran and recommended a number of activities. The circular asked the various sections to concentrate immediately on publicizing the general situation of political prisoners in Iran in order to "awaken greater interest in political imprisonment in Iran" in the public opinion of their own countries. Among the suggested actions:

- Publicity in various national and local presses
- Exhibitions to draw attention to the situation in Iran
- Publicity to the links of Iran with its trading partners (many of whom have strong Amnesty International constituencies)
- Helping groups to organize stands and spread information about Iran's arms deals (this information could provide the various sections with useful news "pegs" for publicity)
- Distributing the briefing paper to local trade unions, local newspapers, leading academics, local businesses having links with Iran.

On November 1, 1976, there was another briefing paper,[11] along with another set of recommendations:

- Telegrams of protest
- Resolutions of protest to be passed at a forthcoming conference
- Formal visits to Iranian embassies, to express concern over the human rights situation
- Special attention to be paid to December 10th, Human Rights Day, the date for launching Prisoner of Conscience Year, plans having been made for inviting several ex-prisoners to an international press conference to be held in London.

I remember how successful this campaign was, how it gained rapidly, how effectively it was used by opposition groups, who had no commitment to the issue of human rights, but who recognized it as a powerful weapon with which to fight the Shah. By the end of 1976, there was a furor about human rights in Iran: one would think these rights were respected everywhere and that Iran's government had a unique and callous disregard of them. It is difficult to escape the conclusion that the Shah's government was singled out by this campaign, not to improve the lot of Iranian political prisoners, but to create a climate in which my brother could be overthrown. I have always thought it strange that this campaign accelerated during the very period when my brother was making his strongest efforts to clean house, to remedy whatever abuses existed.

Universal Human Rights ranked my brother's government at 22nd in a list of per capital political prisoners. Many other countries in our region (Pakistan, Syria, Yemen) and elsewhere ranked higher, yet they were not spotlighted by the press.

December of 1976: Martin Ennals Secretary General of AI made a visit to New York, where the General Assembly of the UN was in session, about to launch the International Year of Prisoners of Conscience. Ennals contacted Fereydoun Hoveyda, our Ambassador and asked to visit Iran. The visit was arranged and my brother received Ennals and an AI team, who subsequently toured our country's prisons. In AI's annual report for

1978, covering the period of June 1977 to June 1978, I found the following: "Some allegations of torture have been received during the last year, but AI has not been able to substantiate them." The organization also found that there had been two political executions during this period: one for the murder of a U.S. Embassy official, the other for espionage for the Soviets.

I remember that I found in this same report the following on our neighbors in Iraq: "Torture allegations are frequent and almost all those who are arrested are reported to be tortured. The bodies of those who are executed, when returned to their families, frequently bear the marks of torture, and deaths under torture are reported." The report also listed the execution of 200 Kurds, 7 communists, 21 military men and one Jordanian. Yet there were no protests approaching the magnitude of those staged against the Shah. The media virtually ignored these and other findings which related to other nations and continued to condemn Iran.

Early in 1977, my brother was beginning to liberalize political life in Iran. Many prisoners were pardoned and General Nassiri, head of SAVAK was removed from office. Bazargan (who became Khomeini's first prime minister) reactivated his Human Rights Committee and circulated documents against the regime. Writers and lawyers followed suit. The opposition was allowed to grow and flourish. Yet little of this was reported in the West. Nor did our new relationship with AI diminish the vehemence of attacks on our regime.

Why did so few voices raise questions about the nature and intent of the unremitting campaign against the Shah? I still have an article written by Alan Hart for the *London Times* (June 9, 1977): "Iran: In Search of Democracy." Hart, a former foreign correspondent for the British Independent News, wrote this after seven months of investigative research in Iran: "To have access to one of Iran's most 'notorious' jails, and the freedom to talk with Iranian political prisoners, including some of who are supposed to be dead, murdered by torture, is an interesting experience for any reporter. But my experience in Evin Prison was only one of many, during seven months of detailed search and investigation ... that caused me to question not merely the accuracy of the allegations made about that country by such organizations as Amnesty International and the International Commission of Jurists, but also the motivation of some of those who are so successful in persuading the media of the free world to accept that Iran is a police state and the Shah some kind of monster." Among the prisoners which Hart interviewed and filmed were those frequently named by the media as being dead or maimed by torture. "One who returned from the dead to be interviewed on film was Dr. Simin Salehi," he wrote. "She was eight months pregnant when she was arrested for taking part in terrorist activities. According to Iranian student organizations in Europe and the USA, Marxist propaganda and the media, Dr. Salehi and the baby died under torture in Evin ... another well known case is that of Sadegh Zibakalam Mofred ... (who) was arrested when delivering funds to terrorist groups in Iran." Hart went on to say that he had "the impression that a great deal of nonsense is talked and written about the Shah," adding that "what the Shah is actually trying to do, at considerable risk to his throne and his life, is to create the institutions for a demo-cratic style of government ... The signs are that if he fails or is not allowed to succeed, his country will collapse.

These were prophetic words, for of course my brother was not allowed to succeed. In fact, the pressure to remove him mounted with each step he took towards liberalization.

March 1977: I shared my growing apprehension about this pressure and talked about it with my brother. He shrugged and said: "This isn't the first time the West has attacked me per-sonally. Remember what happened in 1957, after we signed a contract with Enrico Mattei (the Italian oil czar who agreed to give Iran a 75% share of profits, thus displacing the big oil com-panies)? A campaign was waged against me then and in the western press..."

"But Mattei died a long time ago."

"Yes ... and I'm sure you remember the circumstances," he said quietly, referring to the mysterious and suspicious condi-tions surrounding Mattei's death. "The objectives of the oil companies have not changed. I am too independent to suit them, and they would still like me out."

"That is clear, but I am very concerned about Carter's constant insistence on the human rights issue. It feeds and encourages the opposition ... it tells them that you do not have the support of an ally."

"All the more reason to speed up our reforms," he said. "We have established the basis for economic democracy. Now, if I have the time, I want to see *political* democracy. I'm thinking of a first for Iran ... free elections in the summer of 1979, with the participation of all parties, except perhaps the Tudeh. I've discussed this with my aides..." This conversation still haunts me, for of course my brother knew he was ill. Keeping the news of his illness to himself, he hoped to lay the groundwork for a constitutional monarchy, to prepare the way for an orderly accession to power by his son. At the time his words did little to ease my apprehension. Memories of past crises came back to me: The Mossadegh years and nationalization of the Anglo-Iranian Oil Company; the Mattei episode and the subsequent campaign against Iran. The exploitation of our oil resources—the question of who would profit and to what extent—had been of incredible significance in shaping our history. I thought of the contract with the consortium which operated our oil fields after the nationalization of the AIOCl. Negotiations with the consortium were due to start in the fall, to consider the transfer of all operations to Iran, after the expiration of the present contract (in 1985). Was our political history, once again, being manipulated to serve the interests of the oil industry?

Summer, 1977: I talked to my brother once again about a strange new development. While the campaign against our government was intensifying, the terrorist activities of the Mujahiddin suddenly ceased. At the same time, a number of old politicians who had not been heard from in years suddenly materialized and once more became active. I thought these changes seemed ominous. "Something is in the air," my brother agreed. "These people (the opposition) are trying to outbid me, to escalate their demands with each concession. I think they are not concerned with political negotiation or with human rights. It is clear they will settle for nothing less than the overthrow of our regime. What concerns me most," he added, "is this renewal of the alliance between the Red and the Black." (Separately, these two factions had long been a source of agitation in Iran. The forces of the left, under the influence of 19th century Marxist philosophy opposed the Shah on the grounds of materialism. On the other hand, the Black opposed our country's progressive march forward on obscurantist and narrowly interpreted religious grounds. To them, such measures as land reform, worker participation in profits, liberation of women and universal education are anathema. This coalition had existed once before. In the 1940s the religious fanatics had joined forces with the Tudeh communists. At the beginning of the fifties, the Tudeh waited for Mossadegh to oust the Shah, to create an opportunity for them to take power.)

Later, my brother said: "My intelligence reports speak of a rapprochement within the confederation of students, between the communists and the religious. Their old politicians are surfacing ... encouraged by the declarations of the American President and his aides on the issues of human rights ...."

"Then we must do something," I urged, bringing up, not for the first time, the issue of a counter-campaign in the media. He refused flatly, as he had done before. Propaganda, he said, was a waste of resources. "My people know what I have done for them," he said simply. After observing the success of the campaign to discredit him, the power of media techniques in shaping the minds of people, I was unable to agree. I felt that his accomplishments were being obscured by the skillful and sophisticated use of misinformation techniques to create and manipulate an emotional climate he could not survive.

During that summer of 1977, many underground papers made virulent personal attacks. But the government would not let me respond. In retrospect, it appears that the opposition felt they could attack the Shah by attacking me, that some of our own officials, having made personal accommodations with the opposition, allowed this to happen. Meanwhile, the liberalization continued, the campaign against by brother mounted. It was as if his opponents feared the liberalization program. At that time the religious establishment began to criticize what they called a "permissive society," not in line with "Islamic standards." In the bazaar, the merchants refused to serve female customers who did not wear the veil. In the mosques, the clerics openly criticized all the reforms devised by my brother.

Looking back, I realize that I could see (though western observers often did not), that the reactionary position of the clerics was not based solely on religious precepts, but on some very pragmatic considerations; free elections would result in a further erosion of the power and influence of the clergy. The clergy raised similar objections in 1924, when my father, who admired the accomplishments of Ataturk, wanted to establish a republic in Iran. At that time, the mullahs opposed this move and clung to the monarchy. Traditionally, the clergy of Iran has been against democracy and against education.

It was during this critical summer of 1978 that yet another historical theme repeated itself. The BBC, in its Persian language broadcast, virtually became Khomeini's spokesman. To an outsider this may not have seemed terribly significant. But to us in Iran, the BBC has had, from its inception in 1941, for the express purpose of removing my father from his throne, tremendous political and psychological significance. Since the 19th Century, the British, after their penetration into India, have had an active interest in the internal affairs of Iran. They established solid links with the clergy, who were very powerful within the feudal system of our country. (When I was quite young, there was a popular saying that if you lifted a mullah's beard, you would find the slogan "Made in England.") The British presence in our internal affairs became even stronger after they had obtained the concession for our southern oil fields. The Anglo-Iranian Oil Company became, in fact, a state within a state. After my father's reforms, their influence became more indirect. Even though World War II diminished the power of England, its prestige and psychological influence remained strong in Iran, where the people attribute a great deal of what happens to

British intrigues. During the War and later, the BBC acquired a particular and symbolic importance in the minds of Iranians and other inhabitants of the Persian Gulf countries. The British, aware of this, have often used the BBC (in spite of repeated disclaimers as to the stations' independence of official foreign policy) to further particular political causes. The fact that the BBC had suddenly become a forum for the mullahs did not go unnoticed. At all levels of society, people began to wonder if they were witnessing a reprise of the time when the British (through the BBC) made known to the citizens of Iran that their ruler, my father Reza Khan, must go. They had a growing sense of the power of the campaign against my brother—and they saw his liberalization measures, his unwillingness to muzzle the opposition as a sign of weakness.

During the last months of 1977, the tone of the BBC broadcasts became increasingly inflammatory, reflecting the alliance between "Red and Black." In 1978 the BBC stationed a number of stringers throughout Iran. As soon as an incident would occur in some remote part of the country, the BBC would, a few hours later, broadcast gory accounts of alleged government atrocities in its Persian language program, generally without checking the accuracy of their information. Propagandists like Ibrahim Yazdi were given hours of air time to make speeches attacking the Shah, but our government was never given the opportunity to respond. By late fall, after Khomeini's departure from Iraq and his installation in Paris, the BBC was broadcasting his long, ranting speeches, his calls for the overthrow of the government in their entirety.

Members of my brother's government began to refer to the BBC as "Public Enemy Number One," and on November 30, 1978, a member of our parliament raised the issue: "A glance at the events and developments throughout the world over the past year demonstrates a diabolical plan aimed at the disintegration of Iran... You should not be surprised if you see that the BBC prepares programs and during its three programs in Persian thinks of nothing but to make provocations, create disturbances and chaos. This old fox Britain, no longer able to secure good for itself, is looking for a prey. My question to the government is: Why does it not clarify political facts, and why does it not inform the people about political developments in the world which have been launched against Iran? Why does the government unveil England's design, while it is still tasting the fruits of its plunderings?"

I know very well that the BBC came to function more and more as a coordinator for the various factions seeking to overthrow the Shah. Through the BBC, Tehran's mullahs were able to organize simultaneous demonstrations in cities hundreds of miles apart. In Paris, Khomeini launched his campaign by cassette, making tapes ordering his followers to rampage through the streets. Within hours, these tapes would be broadcast in Iran from the BBC's London headquarters. Few voices questioned what was happening. In November 1978, Robert Moss, columnist for the *Daily Telegraph* and editor of the Economist's influential and confidential weekly *Foreign Report*, published a study called: "The Campaign to Destabilize Iran" (The Institute for the Study of Conflict, London, 1978). Moss described the Soviet Union's interest in destabilizing the Gulf area and the international anti-Shah campaign. In his discussion of 'reactions to foreign broadcasts,' he said: "Somewhat surprisingly, official Soviet broadcasts have taken a carefully moderate and factual line in their reporting... Potent though the Soviet time on the air, Iranian officials know that the BBC's Farsi-language service has exercised exceptional influence throughout the disturbances... They feel themselves entitled to what they consider unbiased treatment from their friends... The BBC's Overseas Service—balanced and comprehensive news coverage without fear or favor has in the particular circumstances of Iran had unfortunate consequences—Farsi speakers in Tehran do offer some specific examples of what they contend to be serious distortions in the coverage of events in Iran. On September 25th, quoting its own correspondent in Tehran, the BBC comments on the handling of the earthquake disaster in Tabbas, that 'public criticism of the government's handling of the earthquake are widespread. Most help has been provided by civilian and religious leaders. The religious people include those who opposed the Shah in recent demonstrations.' (The BBC) gave lengthy coverage on October 23rd to a report by the left-wing Labour MP, Mr. Russell Kerr, member of a team who arrived at the conclusion that 'in the eyes of thousands of Iranians the Shah's regime is illegal.' These are specimens of the sort of things that Farsi-speaking British residents of Tehran, as well as the Iranian government, have been complaining about."

I remember that although the BBC insisted on its objectivity whenever my brother would, through his ambassador, register a protest, it did not hesitate to broadcast unfounded rumors—like the abdication of the Shah (early in December 1978) or his assassination (mid-December). Iranians became convinced that the British wanted the Shah out—and that just as before, their wishes would prevail. The decisive influence of the London broadcasts has been noted by John Stempel, head of the political section of the U.S. Embassy in Tehran: "One international factor did boost the growing opposition movement. The BBC's Persian Service, for three decades considered by both the establishment and the opposition as 'must' listening for international news and juicy Iranian items, began reporting extensively on dissident activities in the fall of 1977. By December the government was referring to the BBC as 'Public Enemy Number One' and protesting the broadcast of so much inflammatory material by the external service of a longtime ally. It also increased the Shah's suspicions of Britain and, by extension, the United States. There is no doubt that expatriate Iranians sympathetic to the revolution effectively captured the Persian Service of the BBC. While wrapping themselves in the flag of freedom of speech, they proceeded to turn their broadcasts into an extension of the opposition's communications network. This gave the opposition movement pronouncements and versions of international events legitimacy."[12]

What I can see now is that expatriate Iranians could not have "captured" the BBC without the complicity of the British government. In fact the opposition had captured most of the western media and by distorting the image of our government, as well as the image of what would follow if the Shah were over-thrown. In the preface of a recent book on the "Islamic experiment," the authors discuss their visit to Neauphle-le-Chateau on New Year's Eve, 1978: "There, in a room decorated only with Persian carpets and with the cuckoo clock the former French tenant had apparently left behind, a constant crowd awaited a glimpse of the leader, engaged in heated debates with clerics and fantasized about the future. Ibrahim Yazdi was there to instruct the Imam's followers on the proper mode of inter-acting with the Western press: 'Be sure to stress three points,' he told them. 'The rights of minorities, the rights of women, and the holding of elections.'" These points and other issues of "rights" of all kinds were stressed and promised by the opposi-tion, in their search for powerful allies and media support. Now, of course, these issues are forgotten, discarded, along with the allies, now that power has been achieved.

Today, as these same authors point out, many formerly prominent Iranians of various political persuasion, are dead, dis-graced or imprisoned. Tens of thousands of displaced Iranians: intellectuals, technocrats, business people, all of various shad-ings of political thought (including outspoken critics of the Shah) try to "rally their energies and understand what had happened." In the years since Khomeini's mullahs took power, there have been some interesting shadings in the way in which the media covers Iran. There appears to be an almost universal embar-rassment about the tens of thousands of words, most of it misinformation and misinterpretation, that were written about my brother's reign and about the "holy" man from Qum. When stories of atrocity and terror appear, there is an absence of the kind of editorializing seen so often in the past. Furthermore, there seems to be a need to find some good in the present re-gime, so words like "stability" appear in describing the reign of the mullahs, in spite of growing evidence that time is running out for this Islamic Republic.

2: KHOMEINI SPINS HIS WEB

KHOMEINI IN EXILE: Recently I had an interesting visit with a former student of theology, a man who described to me his personal experience of hearing Khomeini teach in Najef, Iraq, in 1966. At the end of a back street, young bearded men wearing brown 'abas' slowly entered the paved courtyard of a traditional Arab house. They made their way to the first room. After removing their shoes, they bowed reverently to the old man sitting cross-legged on a small rug. His bald head was hidden by a black skull cap, a full beard covered most of his face. Staring fixedly into space, he barely acknowledged the salaams of his pupils. The young mullahs sat around him, forming a half-circle.

"Islam," the old man began in a monotone, "is the religion of fighters who claim both right and justice, of those who demand freedom and independence, of those who do not accept the domination of believers by infidels. The fulfillment of Islam demands the creation of an Islamic state, true and pure. Allah has given orders for the organization of society and the respect of his laws. Islam has precepts for everything regarding men and society. These rules came from the Almighty and were transmitted to men by the Prophet. We are marveled by the loftiness of these commandments which cover all aspects of life, from the conception of man to his death and burial... There are no subjects left on which Islam has not established rules. A set of laws

19

does not suffice to reform society. An executive authority is needed. That is why Allah, praises to him, has not only delivered laws, but also instituted on earth a government with executive and administrative branches. The Prophet, may the benediction of Allah be upon him, has presided on all these branches and ruled the Islamic society in its entirety. He has transmitted and explained the laws and, in addition, has taken care to apply them personally until the constitution of an Islamic state. For example, in his time, the Prophet did not limit himself to dictating a penal code. He also applied and enforced it. He cut off hands, whipped and stoned. Following him, the Khalifs accomplished the same duties. Muslims were new to Islam and needed a superior authority to watch over the full enforcement of laws. It is evident that this need for authority should not limit itself to the time of the Prophet. It continues to exist, for Islam is not by time or location. The Islamic government is submitted to the law of Islam which emanates neither from the people nor from his representatives, but from divine will. The Koranic law, which is divine law, constitutes the very essence of any Islamic government. This law is immutable till the end of time.

"Allah has ordered men to obey the Prophet and his successors. The qualities required for executive authority exist only in the person of the Faquihs (ulemas). It is the task of a recognized Faquih to create and direct an Islamic government. It is the duty of citizens to obey him. The Faquihs were designated by Allah to direct men. In Islam, to govern means to put into practice Koranic laws which must be obeyed by all without exception and unquestioningly. The agents of colonialism and imperialism have injected their poison into the minds of educated people. All traces of intellectualism and colonialist aggression must be wiped out. It is a full century since western medicine and surgery were introduced in Iran. Our so-called leaders went so far as to forget our traditional medicine in order to encourage young, inexperienced people in the way of this accursed European medicine, and now today we realize that diseases such as typhus can only be cured by ancient traditional methods. We only have one means at our disposal in order to secure the unity of the Islamic community and liberate our Islamic fatherland: The establishment of a true Islamic government, the uprooting of all tyrannical pseudo-Muslim governments created by foreign hands. Once our goal is achieved, we must work for the establishment of a universal Islamic government. Holy war means the conquest of non-Muslim territories. It can be declared following the establishment of a truly Islamic government under the direction of the Imam or upon his orders. The final end is to have Koranic law ruling this planet from one end to the other. The entire world must understand that hegemony of Islam differs from all others. Thus an Islamic government must be created under the authority of the Imam, in order that he may start this war, which differentiates itself from all other tyrannical and unjust wars of conquest, for those disregard the high moral and civilizing principles of Islam." (These precepts can all be found in Khomeini's books, *An Islamic Government* and *Secrets Revealed*).

Who is this strange man who, unlike other ayatollahs, speaks only of politics and power and conquest? Among his peers, he is the least cultured, the least erudite. In the religious hierarchy, he ranks below a Taleghani or a Shariat-Madari. His thinking is convoluted, his ramblings verbose, self-contradicting and often hysterical. But he is a stubborn and tenacious man, animated with a spirit of vengeance. Born with the century, he grew-up in Khomeini, the village where his parents immigrated and from which he took his name. He was taught to read and write by a mullah, and later, he went to Qum (a holy city) to study theology. After his religious training, Khomeini returned to his native village, where his ascetic ways brought him followers from neighboring villages. The death of his father brought him a substantial inheritance of real estate holdings, which made him a well-to-do and independent mullah.

There is a good deal more to tell about Khomeini following the second World War. It was then that he became close to Ayatollah Kashani, who had just founded the Fedayeen Islam, a terrorist organization. (Kashani built a strong following among the "mafia" of the bazaar, the so-called "drawers of knives," and with their support, could produce "instant" mobs to take a "pro" or "anti" stance on almost any issue—a lesson Khomeini learned well.) The ideas of this fighting priest fascinated Khomeini, and this period marked his growing interest in politics. As a young mullah, he had this to say (these words would be repeated thirty years later): "All laws approved by the parliament must be abolished. Obey God and those among you who hold the divine authority. The only government accepted by Allah on the day of the resurrection must be organized according to divine laws and that is only possible under the total control of the mullahs."

Yet for all of his interest in politics, I find it odd that Khomeini stayed in the background during the troubled Mossadegh years. He surfaced in 1962, when the reforms of the White Revolution began, inciting his partisans to revolt against modernization, land reform and the emancipation of women. His support came from a segment of the clergy which was alarmed by the distribution, to the peasants, of tillable land, 20% of which had been managed by the mullahs. His fiery speeches provoked uprisings. He attacked the various reforms and the discarding of the veil as un-Islamic and denounced the *de facto* relationship between Iran and Israel. In a message to the officers of the Imperial Army, he said: "I know their (officers') hearts are troubled...subordination to Israel, and that they don't wish Iran to be trampled by the boots of the Jews." At that time, he spoke neither of democracy nor social justice, as he would do later at Neauphle-le-Chateau in France. Following an upheaval in the Tehran bazaar, he was detained, but my brother reprieved and exiled him in 1963. He went first to Turkey (where he was unwelcome) and then settled in Najaf, the holy city of Shiism in Iraq. There he developed his ideas and lectured to young local mullahs, as well as those from Iran. He urged the necessity of revolt against the Shah's regime, as well as those of all the Persian Gulf rulers. He gave no timetable for this goal, and those who asked, he quoted the Koran: "O thou who believes. Ask for the aid of patience and prayer. Allah is with those who are patient." (II, 153). An idea obsessed him: to revenge himself on the Shah whose government took his land and dispossessed him (later, he would add to his revenge list the government of Saddam Hussein, which forced him out of Iraq). And since a personal quarrel cannot be the primer of a general movement, he assembled a theory of Islamic government gathered from the history of Islam and rearranged to support his personal goals. He attempted to follow the lead of Ayatollah Kashani, who used a terrorist organization and a network of mullahs to capture the presidency of the Parliament under Mossadegh, but failed to create a similar network. The great majority of clergy were not interested in revolt against the Shah, who provided them with substantial subsidies and the opportunities to criticize some of his reforms. Failing to find a following among the mullahs in Iran, Khomeini turned to the other Islamic states.

In fact what Khomeini did was to export an Imam to Lebanon. The Arab world, with its Sunni majority, does not subscribe to the idea of an Imam as supreme guide. It leans instead toward nationalism of the Nasserian type, so that Khomeini decided to build a power base of the Shi'ite minorities, who would, he calculated, be receptive to his ideas. The largest single bloc of Shi'ites is found in Lebanon: One million people, most of them downtrodden and disinherited. It was here that he began his operation. In Najaf, he was able to plot freely, for Iraq was at the time still entangled in a territorial dispute with Iran—and therefore hospitable to my brother's opponents. From Najaf, Khomeini sent to Lebanon one of his friends, Musa Sadr, an Iranian who was fluent in Arabic and a skilled orator. The ayatollah's envoy rapidly gained ascendancy over the Lebanese Shi'ites and became their Imam. In the early 70s, the time was right for another alliance. Yasser Arafat's Palestinians had been driven from Jordan, in the aftermath of a power struggle with King Hussein's army. The most important fighting factions, the PLO and head of Fattah, thought it good policy to form close ties with the Shi'ites, who were in the majority in south Lebanon. Musa Sadr also saw the value of an alliance. His AMAL organization was political, he lacked a fighting organization and it was Arafat who could provide him with one. Politically, the two groups had much in common: the Palestinians were principally Muslim; they were opposed to western and American imperialism; they were fighting against the occupation of their lands by Israel. Sadr proposed the alliance to his mentor, and Khomeini agreed that ties with Arafat would be beneficial to his plans for an Islamic revolution. To a Palestinian journalist, he declared: "The men of the Fattah movement must be supported and aided with all resources and capabilities. The Muslim Palestinian's duty is the duty of every Muslim in every part of the world."[14]

And so it was that Fattah signed an agreement with the Shi'ites. It brought to Khomeini its organizational experience; aided Musa Sadr's AMAL group in creating a militia; trained (in its camps) Iranians in guerrilla fighting and street demonstrations; taught civilians the rudiments of political agitation. Still another alliance was forged between Musa Sadr and Syria's Hafez Assad, an Alawite, and ideologically closer to the Shi'ites than the Sunnis. (Later, in 1976, when Syria occupied a part of war torn Lebanon, Sadr would offer considerable help.) By the early '70s, the PLO-Khomeini-Syria axis came into being.

These new developments were well known to our secret service. In Iran it has always been possible to buy mullahs (indeed foreign powers conducted an active trade in mullahs since before my father's time), and so our government made contact with Musa Sadr. Sadr requested financial assistance for his "organization of the disinherited" and other projects involving Lebanese Shi'ites. As an Iranian, he knew we could not offer him arms, which would have been used by the PLO. After several meetings with our ambassador in Beirut, however, it was agreed that Iran would give him a first installment of one million dollars. Shortly thereafter, Sadr muted his criticisms of my brother's government, and for a period of time, he cooperated closely with our agents in Lebanon. I do not know how he explained this change of position to Khomeini, but it was relatively short-lived. A few months later, the second installment disappeared in transit, between Beirut and south Lebanon. We never learned what happened to this money. Some speculated that it was intercepted by Israeli agents, while others theorized that it was taken by Arafat's people. Sadr accused Iran of failing to keep its commitment and resumed his attacks on the Shah. Our regime also attempted to establish better relations with the PLO and with Syria's President Assad, who visited Tehran and obtained considerable economic aid from the Shah. However, this did not slow the revolutionary activities of the PLO/Syria/Sadr group.

As the journalist Alpher wrote in the *Washington Quarterly* (Autumn 1980):

"Beginning in the early seventies, the Syria-PLO connection brought together several thousand Iranian Mujahedeens and Fedayi (Islamic-Marxists and Marxists) guerrillas for training in the Fattah camps in Lebanon and Syria; it also assembled a number of capable Iranian exiles. They had two things in common: a desire to depose the Shah and recognition of Khomeini's leadership. Together the exiles, the Syrians and the Palestinians, prepared cadres for revolutionary activities inside Iran. They organized arms smuggling operations into the country, using food transport trucks leaving Beirut to conceal weapons and explosives. They recruited supporters for the pro-Khomeini student movement which they organized throughout the Middle-East, Western Europe and the United States. They prepared and infiltrated propaganda and agitators back into Iran. They were free to move about Lebanon and Syria, visit Libya and Algeria, and organize a revolution. The clandestine nature of their movements at this time makes their activities difficult to reconstruct. But enough details about some of the principal figures involved have been brought to light by Arab and Iranian sources to paint at least a partial picture."

In addition to these important connections, Khomeini acquired, over the years, a number of secular and religious allies, who would later play an important part in the Islamic Republic:

Abol-Hassan Bani-Sadr: The former president of the Islamic Republic is the son of an ayatollah who had close ties with Khomeini. Bani-Sadr participated in the disturbances of 1963. My brother allowed him to leave the country (after falling out of favor with Khomeini he was obliged to flee for his life). He settled in Paris, where he lived the life of a "professional student," publishing a few pamphlets and an anti-Shah book titled *Petrole et Violence*. At that time he presented himself as an intellectual, with a particular interest in economic theories, rather than as a practicing revolutionary. In 1972, he went to Najaf for his father's funeral. He renewed his acquaintance with Khomeini, and after an exchange of ideas, he began to correspond regularly with the old ayatollah. Like the other seculars, he served as a bridge between the West (and particularly the U.S.) and Khomeini, helping to present the old man in a moderate light and counseling him in matter of public image. Once the Shah had been removed and the Republic established, Bani-Sadr, like the other seculars, found that Khomeini's earlier flexibility had vanished. Later, in exile, he would complain, that his plans to ease the country's food shortages by purchases abroad was violently opposed by the ayatollah, who accused Bani-Sadr of sabotaging the revolution by cheating the people of the "experience of deprivation"[15]. During his association with Khomeini, Bani-Sadr was apparently converted to the use of political terror, for following his flight from Iran in 1981, he declared that he had ordered his partisans to "gun down" the five leaders of the Republic (Rafsanjani, Rajai, Bahonar, Ardebili, Mahdavi-Kani). "If these five persons were to be killed tonight," he said, "the government of Khomeini would collapse."

Mustafa Chamran: Left Iran in 1957, to attend the University of California at Berkeley. He was an avowed communist and closely cooperated with students of the Tudeh Party. In 1963, he went to Egypt, where he received military training and participated in anti-Iranian activities ordered by President Nasser (he was visited in Cairo on several occasions by Sadegh Ghotzbadeh and Ibrahim Yazdi). When our government resumed diplomatic relations with Egypt, Chamran went to south Lebanon and contributed to the creation of Musa Sadr's AMAL militia (just as he would later help create Khomeini's Revolutionary Guards). He was a part of Sadr's liaison with the PLO, and he participated in the military training of Iranian students. For a time, he still aired Marxist ideas, but soon converted to Islamic fundamentalism. In 1979, he returned to Iran, together with a number of PLO specialists, and was nominated Minister of Defense before the war with Iraq. Chamran died on the front lines, some say from bullet wounds in the back. According to lingering rumors in Iran, he was assassinated on orders from the mullahs.

Jalaladin Farsi: An Iranian of Afghani descent, he went to Lebanon about the same time as Chamran. He joined the PLO and quickly became an officer. In 1978, he secretly returned to Iran to help organize anti-government riots and the formation of a revolutionary militia. The *Journal de Teheran* announced, on February 27, 1979: "It is said that Jalaladin Farsi, an Iranian who for years was a militant in Palestinian organizations, where he commanded a battalion, will be the head of the Revolutionary Guards. His unit has trained many Iranian fighters, some of whom were killed in the course of combat with Israel, while other organized the nucleus of the armed resistance against the Shah."

Sadegh Ghotzbadeh: Like Bani-Sadr, this son of a furniture merchant was for many years a "professional student." He left Iran in 1959 and drifted through several American, Canadian and European universities. In the U.S., he made contact with Professor Richard Cottam* of Pittsburgh University and organized anti-Shah demonstrations. After being expelled by the U.S.,

---

*In his book, *All Fall Down* (New York, Random House, 1985), Gary Sick writes that "Professor Cottam maintained close contact with Iranian opposition figures, and he argued that Khomeini's positions—apart from his absolute opposition to the Shah—were relatively moderate and deserved a hearing." (p. 54) Sick discusses Cottam's efforts to arrange meetings between Ibrahim Yazdi (whom he describes as "a key figure in organizing and directing the anti-Shah activities or Iranian students and citizens in the United States") and members of the State Department and the National Security Council, since it is well known that Cottam worked for the intelligence community, his role as spokesman and intermediary for the opposition raises some questions.

he went to Lebanon, where he received revolutionary training in Palestinian camps. Later came a period of clandestine activities, using a newspaper distribution agency in Beirut as cover, and a Syrian passport provided by Musa Sadr's contacts. Some of Ghotzbadeh's missions involved transporting Libyan funds to Khomeini's supporters in Iran. During the Lebanese civil war, he actively helped the PLO. In 1973 he moved to Paris, to replace Mahmud Hamshari, the assassinated PLO representative. In Paris, he began to move in leftist circles, but after joining Khomeini at Neauphle le-Chateau, he sent a letter to the French magazine *L'Express*,[16] denying any communist sympathies.

I will always remember this man who, as Khomeini's Minister of Foreign Affairs, advised Hamilton Jordan to have my brother murdered as a means of resolving the hostage crisis. Later, when he was accused of plotting against Khomeini, he asked for mercy, but was executed by the mullahs in 1982. Upon learning of Ghotzbadeh's death, Jimmy Carter referred to him as "a real hero in the hostage crisis." It struck me then that only Carter could choose a hero like Ghotzbadeh.

Ibrahim Yazdi: This son of a rich bazaar merchant was a militant during the fifties in Mossadegh's nationalist movement. After Mossadegh fell, Yazdi joined the "Front for Resistance," created by Ayatollah Taleghani and Mehdi Bazargan. In 1960, he emigrated to the U.S., continued his studies and worked as a researcher in Houston and became an American citizen. He made contact with a number of university professors, including Cottam and organized the "Association of Iranian Islamic Students." During his frequent trips to Europe and the Middle East, he visited Ghotzbadeh, Chamran and Khomeini. In 1972, the ayatollah named him as his personal representative to the U.S. In this capacity, he became Khomeini's spokesman and intermediary to members of the American government. In 1978, he joined Khomeini at Neauphle-le-Chateau and later returned with him to Iran in February 1979. He was an active member of the Iranian Revolutionary Council, participating in the mass mock trials which condemned to death virtually everyone who had in any way been associated with our government. Later he became

Minister for Foreign Affairs in Bazargan's cabinet, and after the Bazargan government fell, he entered the Parliament. Under constant attacks from the mullahs, he was forced to retire from the political scene, as was his son-in-law Shahriar Rouhani, who served briefly as Khomeini's representative to the United States.

Mehdi Bazargan: Son of an Azerbaijani merchant, he was sent to Europe in 1927 on an educational scholarship granted by my father Reza Shah. He received an engineering degree in France and became a full-time professor at Tehran University. By 1942, he had created, at the University, an anti-communist "Islamic Society," which Ibrahim Yazdi, then a young student, joined. In 1952, Bazargan collaborated with the Mossadegh government, and after that regime fell, he formed an underground organization, the "Iranian Freedom Movement." Within this group he attempted to unite members of the bazaar and the clergy with intellectual democrats. As the head of an engineering company, he had a following among other educated Iranians. In 1977, during my brother's liberalization program, he formed a Committee for Human Rights. Through Yazdi, Ghotzbadeh and Chamran, he remained in close touch with Khomeini, without openly affiliating himself with the ayatollah. Under the influence of his associates, Bazargan was convinced that Khomeini's leadership was necessary in order to bring about a change in regime. For Khomeini, these secular politicians were necessary for a time, though he considered them guilty of introducing to Islamic countries all the turpitude of the West. As Alpher says:

"As for Khomeini, he needed the politicians for several practical reasons. During the struggle he calculated that it was better to be allied to them than to be antagonistic towards them. If the Shah were to appoint one of them prime minister, for example, it would delay Khomeini's rise to power. Moreover, they could give the anti-Shah movement respectability and appeal in the West; the international media found it much easier to establish a rational dialogue with them than with Khomeini. They could be used to weaken a vital source of the Shah's support. Lastly, (there were) the technocrats whom Khomeini had long planned to use to help run his Islamic regime—devoid of real power, but knowledgeable in the working of civil service systems, hospital networks, transportation, communications and all other accouterments of modernity which even the mullahs found useful." These people Khomeini deceived for a time, with conciliatory language and an apparent willingness to negotiate and compromise. Those he considered his true allies, however, were some of the backward but highly activist clergy in Iran. The most prominent of these were:

Muhammad-Hussain Beheshti: who died in an explosion at the "Islamic Party" center, received his doctorate in theology from the University of Tehran, under the tutelage, of Ayatollah Taleghani. Unlike Khomeini's other religious allies, he participated in no anti-Shah activities prior to 1978. On the contrary, he cooperated closely with our government, particularly with the SAVAK, for which he received a considerable salary. For a time, he served as spiritual head of the Shi'ite community in West Germany and resided in Hamburg. Several of the students he supervised during that period have told me that he never discussed Iranian politics, except to praise the Shah's reforms. When he returned to Iran, he became the official supervisor of school texts and manuals—which could not be printed without his seal of approval. His function was to assure the government that all textbooks were in accordance with the principles of Islam. (Later, when our Minister of Education, Mrs. Farrokhrou Parsa, was accused by the Revolutionary Council of ignoring the teachings of Islam in school textbooks, she tried to explain that all books were printed with the blessings of his eminence Beheshti. She was dragged from the court, beaten and executed on the spot.) Beheshti also had numerous business interests, including a construction and import-export company. (Later, when his enemies pointed to his commercial activities, he would try to pass these off as charitable institutions.)

I spent some time with Beheshti during my official visit to West Germany in 1967, when he attended a reception given for me at the Iranian consulate in Hamburg. He spoke fluent German and some English, and it was said at the time that he had many friends in London. (I was told that his "untimely and tragic demise" caused some consternation among British officials, including Sir Anthony Parsons.) Nevertheless, I think it was only in 1978 that he became one of the pillars of Khomeini's clandestine organization. Having the protection of SAVAK, he was able to freely receive the tapes of Khomeini's inflammatory speeches, make thousands of copies and distribute them without fear of interference. When Khomeini returned to Tehran, Beheshti emerged as the strong man of the new regime. He founded the Islamic Republican Party, which promptly and efficiently suppressed all opposition by terror and intimidation. He stifled the seculars with gangs of hoodlums calling themselves Hezbollahis (members of the party of Allah). It was Beheshti who placed his own men in positions of power: Rafsanjani, as head of Parliament and Rajai, as head of government. It was also Beheshti who ruined Bani-Sadr and who, as President of the Supreme Court, executed (or assassinated) all those who knew of his association with my brother's regime. Beheshtils defection to Khomeini raised for me the question of SAVAK, and I confess that even today I do not have a clear picture of what was happening within that organization. When Khomeini returned to Tehran, some of its members and high-ranking officials fled or were executed. But almost the entire organization (including General Hossein Fardust, second in command and my brother's childhood friend) passed with "armes et bagages" to Khomeini. I have spoken with a number of exiles, including former intelligence officers. They tell me that there were several factions within the SAVAK: one which maintained close ties with MOSSAD, while another favored the British Intelligence service. According to my sources, this second group began to shift its alliance to Khomeini's mullahs. And while I do not really know the "how" and "why" of it, I do know that by mid-1978, the SAVAK no longer fulfilled its function and was, in fact, providing my brother's government with false information.

Sadegh Khalkhali: Acquired the reputation of "hanging judge" by personally executing hundreds of persons and condemning to death thousands of others. He portrays himself as a "hero" of the resistance against my brother. And while it is true that he was confined during the Shah's regime, it was not for political reasons. Khalkhali was committed to an insane asylum for sadistic acts, including the strangling of dogs and cats. His reputation has been made by blood and the frightening rhetoric of lunacy. It was he who instituted Islamic tribunals, with express-trials and instant executions. "We have no need for lawyers, appeals and all the western trappings which cost so much," he said. "A trial must not be longer than a few hours and the execution carried out immediately. To feed condemned prisoners is to throw money out the window!" It was also Khalkhali who, in Kurdistan, finished off wounded rebels in their hospital cots, without trial, "to save money," he said. It was he who had my younger son Shahriar assassinated in the streets of Paris. "To tell the truth, we were after his mother," Khalkhali told *Le Point*.

"How could you have made such a mistake?" the reporter asked.
"It was he who fell into our hands."
"Are there still more people left on your black list?"
"All those who cooperated with the past regime. All the corrupt on earth."
"What about Farah Diba?" the reporter asked.
"Squeak," replied Khalkhali with a smile, drawing his thumb across his throat.

The remarkable writer, V.S. Naipual, visited Khalkhali during the course of his research on Islam. Here he describes the meeting:

"He was born in Azerbaijan. His father was a very religious man. His father was a farmer. I asked: 'Did you help your father?'"
"'I was a shepherd when I was a boy.' Then he began to clown. Raising his voice, making a gesture, he said, 'Right now I know how to cut a sheep's head, and the Iranians in the room—including some bodyguards—rocked with laughter."[17]

3: THE SOVIET CONNECTION

THE SOVIET CONNECTION: The Soviets have a long history of intervention in the internal affairs of my country, and there can be no doubt that the movement to destabilize the Iran of the Pahlavis originated in Moscow. This campaign included, since the mid 1960s the participation of the Iranian clergy. I do not believe that the Soviets anticipated the present situation in Iran, any more than did Khomeini's western supporters. I think the intent was to weaken the links between Iran and the U.S. and to render us powerless as the "policeman of the Gulf."

I remember a visit I made to Moscow in April, 1966. As I rode through the streets of the city in a black Zim limousine, traveling through the early morning traffic towards the Soviet Communist Party's Central Committee building, I recalled a similar morning exactly 20 years before. I was riding in a black limousine headed for the Kremlin, where the Secretary General of the Communist Party was to receive me. Although I'm able to maintain a surface calm in the face of difficult situations, I was tense and apprehensive at the prospect of meeting Stalin, whose reputation was awesome and frightening. It was a critical moment in our history, for the Soviet Union was, after the end of World War II, still in control of large portions of our northern provinces, where puppet republics had been established. The situation was quite different this pleasant morning in 1966. After Khrushchev's departure, relations between Iran and the Soviet Union had improved. Brezhnev, the new Secretary-General, was not as intimidating as Stalin, and I had acquired enough political experience through the years to be at ease with Russia's political leaders.

The meeting lasted for an hour and a half. It covered various aspects of the relations between Russia and Iran and was quite amiable. Brezhnev went so far as to speak of my brother in glowing terms. Taking advantage of the relaxed atmosphere, I brought up a question that had troubled me for some time. "Mr. Secretary-General, since you seem satisfied with relations between our two countries, can you tell me why radio stations in your territories broadcast attacks on my brother? The Persian language programs of these stations do not reflect the friendly relations you mentioned a few moments ago."

"Soviet broadcasts are full of praise for Iran," Brezhnev protested.

It was true that the Soviets had ceased their attacks on my country. But two stations, one located in East Germany, the other in Bulgaria, were under the control of the KGB and the Tudeh Party, and systematically propagated misinformation about Iran. Brezhnev continued:

> "The stations you refer to are not within our territory and therefore are not under our control. Why don't you establish relations with these countries and discuss the matter with them? I'm certain they would change their attitude once Iran indicates a desire to develop mutually beneficial relations."

Upon my return to Iran, I reported this exchange to my brother. Eventually we officially recognized East Germany and opened an embassy in Bulgaria. The attacks on our regime ceased almost immediately. I thought the matter settled and was happy to have made a modest contribution in stemming the anti-

Iranian propaganda from these two sources. A year later, I learned, to my dismay, of the KGB and Tudeh involvement in the violent anti-Shah demonstrations in West Berlin. I had thought that the normalization of our relations with the Soviet bloc, the strengthening of our economic ties, would ease certain pressures emanating from the communist bloc. I did not realize then that there was often a dichotomy between "state relations" and "party line."

When my brother returned from a state visit to Germany, I discussed the matter with him. I said indignantly that Brezhnev had cheated me. He laughed and told me it was unrealistic to expect a change in Soviet policy, regardless of our improved relations. "That's why we must always remain vigilant and work towards rapid economic and military development." And indeed he was right. Though Brezhnev, in his speeches, often referred to the relations between our two countries as an example of the good neighbor policy, the objectives of the Soviet Union remained the same. Since the time of Peter the Great, Russia has sought access to the warm-water ports of the Persian Gulf and the Indian Ocean, a goal which the Tsars' successors have never abandoned.

As I was growing up I heard stories of Russia's long involvement in my country. At the turn of the century, Iran was a decaying nation, its glorious past all but forgotten. Tsarist Russia occupied virtually all of the north, while the British exercised their authority over the south, where they just extorted the oil fields of Khuzistan from the Qajar Shahs. In 1907, the two powers, in order to avoid direct confrontations, formalized this de facto situation with an agreement which divided Iran into two zones of influence. The central government in Tehran was a puppet, its strings pulled by foreign powers. The heads of the tribes and the large property owners became increasingly independent of the capital. The bulk of the population lived in abject poverty. The peasants were serfs, subject to the will of the landowners. The mullahs controlled vast land holdings, which were worked by the peasants. Taking advantage of the superstitions of the masses, the mullahs used their influence for their own benefit, as well as for the feudal lords. The illiterate masses considered the mullahs, who could read and write, to be superior beings who relayed the voice of God. This "voice" often had a strong Russian or English accent.

World War I brought great suffering to Iran. The Russians, English and Ottomans invaded. After the Bolshevik revolution of 1917, a certain Kuchik Khan founded a communist republic, under the protection of Lenin, in Guilan, a province on the Caspian Sea. In the early 1920s my father was an officer in the cossack garrison at Ghazvine, a town 130 kilometers from Tehran. He was filled with patriotic anger at the sorry condition of Iran. We, his children, often heard him tell of those days, of how the country was falling apart and how he resolved that something must be done. In 1921, he marched with his battalion into Tehran and took control of the city. Lenin and Rothstein (his Commissioner of Foreign Affairs) deemed it best to support the new central power in Tehran. They abandoned their support of the Persian communists in the north and signed a pact of friendship with Iran. But the Iranian Communist Party, dispersed for the moment, would reform clandestinely several years later. Preoccupied with the internal struggle for power and the consolidation of the new regime after Lenin's death in 1924, the Russians put their ambitions in Iran aside—for the moment. Their hopes for a warm water port were not abandoned, and the next two decades presented the Russians with still more reasons for an active interest in Iran. Experts predicted a future oil deficit in the USSR. World War II demonstrated clearly the strategic value of my country, for it was through Iran that American assistance allowed the Russians to withstand Hitler's formidable assaults.

As I remember it, in 1946, Washington forced the Soviets to withdraw from the north, to abandon their "democratic" puppet regimes in Azerbajian and Kurdistan. This new presence of the U.S., with all its economic and military power, in our region, where only the British had been active before, was a source of great concern to the Soviets. If Iran were to allow American bases on her territory, so close to Russia's borders, these would constitute a serious threat. (In the 1970s this danger became more acute in Soviet eyes, because of the development of sophisticated electronic surveillance devices and refined missiles.) Understandably it has become a major objective of Soviet policy, since World War II, to prevent the U.S. or any other hostile major power (China, for example) from gaining too much influence in Iran. Still another source of concern for the Russians was the fact that their southern republics (Tajikistan, Uzbekistan, etc.) share with us the same culture and religion. In the event of a world war, it would be easy for a hostile Iran to infiltrate these republics and create serious internal problems for the Soviets. For all these reasons, the Russians have, without abandoning their long-term objectives, acted circumspectly in my country. Officially, they sought and welcomed improved relations in the mid-sixties. And they did not, for example, take sides in our border disputes with their client, Iraq. For his part, my brother began his reign with considerable caution where the Soviets were concerned. While seeking normal bilateral relations with them, he took such steps as he could to counter the spread of Soviet influence in our region. He expanded trade exchanges and economic cooperation with the Russians. But at the same time, he continued to purchase arms from the U.S. and to establish friendly ties with China. (I am rather proud of the part I played in paving the way for the recognition of Iran by Communist China, long before the normalization of Sino-American relations. Using personal channels, I obtained an invitation to visit China and meet with its leaders.)

In the early seventies, the masters of the Kremlin followed these developments in my brother's foreign policy, registering a few discreet signs of displeasure at the growth of our arms purchases from the U.S. and the establishment of diplomatic relations with China.

Things became far more complex by 1975, when our Prime Minister, Amir Abbas Hoveyda made a stop at the Moscow aerodrome following a visit to outer Mongolia. Kosegyin informed him of his government's concern over Iran's arms purchases. At about the same time, in New York, Andre Gromyko brought up Iran's stockpiling of military weaponry in a meeting with Abbas Khalatbary, our Minister of Foreign Affairs. Our minister replied that these weapons were not directed against the Soviet Union. Gromyko responded: "Of course, we know that. But we ask ourselves the question: 'Why is Iran arming itself to the teeth?' Who does your country fortify itself against? Iraq? But Iraq is a small country. Against the Gulf Emirates? They do not count on the military level. Against Saudi Arabia? They do not threaten Iran. So we must ask ourselves why?" The same year, during the course of a dinner at our embassy, the Soviet representative took me aside and said: "Our relations have been excellent up to this point, and we, for our part, are trying to further improve them. The Shah has practiced a policy of maintaining the status quo, which we have welcomed. We know the United States has had a privileged position in Iran since the end of the war. We have accepted that reality in our relations with you. But with your insatiable appetite for the most modern, the most advanced armaments, you risk disrupting the very equilibrium you have yourselves created." Similar remarks were made by another Soviet diplomat to our ambassador to the UN. But these remarks were made in otherwise friendly discussions. Behind the scenes, however, the KGB carried on its destabilizing activities, inside Iran and outside, particularly among exiled leftists.

THE KGB IN IRAN: Though the Soviets officially abandoned Iran's communists in 1921, their secret service, then called the Guepeou, planted agents throughout the country who cultivated contacts in diverse areas of our society. Though Russia's communists were proclaimed atheists, they understood very early the importance of ties with our Shi'ite clergy. Like the British before them, they "bought" a number of mullahs.

I have in my files some interesting clippings from Le Matin (Oct. 26-30, 1930), detailing the story of Georges Sergueivitch Agavekev, one of the first Soviet agents in Iran. In 1929, he directed the Guepeou network in our country. The following year, he defected and found asylum in France, where he made the following comments during the course of a lengthy interview: "Our agent in Qum spoke Farsi as well as a native born in the holy city. He had his connections among the mullahs and we were kept apprised, via his intermediary, of the very efficient operations of our English colleagues vis-a-vis the mullahs. Now we have our mullahs, too." Since those early days half a century ago, the Soviets have stepped up, without interruption—even today, under Khomeini—their operations in all segments of our society: the clergy, the administration, the army, etc. Whenever one of their agents is discovered, he is replaced without delay. I have documentation of the career of one such agent, Geider Aliev, who was, in 1982, made a titular member of the Politburo and Vice President of the Council of Ministers. A native of Iran, he was born in Nakhjavan in 1923 and speaks both Farsi and Azari Turkish (Azerbaijani). After perfecting his language skills, he joined the KGB in 1941, with the rank of second lieutenant. In 1945, he was sent to Iran, to control the so-called Democratic Republic of Azerbaijan, created by Iranian communists under the shadow of the Soviet occupation army. One of his initiatives immediately attracted the attention of his superiors: He brought the "Friday Imam" from the mosque in Bakou (in Soviet Azerbaijan) to Tabriz, to exhort the local mullahs to support the puppet republic. Aliev understood quite well the influence of the mullahs on the Iranian masses and would, in the course of his career, use this effectively to achieve Soviet political objectives. A few years later he was posted in Moscow, to coordinate relations with the militants of the Iranian Azerbaijani Party and the Tudeh Party, who had fled to the Soviet Union. In 1958, he met Yuri Andropov, who was then a high-ranking official in the office of the Secretary of the Central Committee of the Party. Aliev succeeded in interesting Andropov in Iranian affairs. With Andropov's help, Aliev installed a radio station in Sofia, Bulgaria, to broadcast propaganda on behalf of Iran's communists, in Farsi and Turkish throughout the Middle East. When Andropov became head of the KGB, he named Aliev chief of operations in Azerbaijan. In this position he maintained contacts with the Tudeh Party, whose leaders were in East Germany. With Andropov's approval, he sent party militants for specialized training to Cuba and to the Palestinian camps in Lebanon, Syria and Libya. Aliev took a special interest in Tudeh Party member Kianouri, a favorite grandson of Mullah. (When Khomeini emerged as the leader of the anti-Shah movement in 1978, Aliev made Kianouri head of the Tudeh Party, by forcing the Secretary-General, Eskandari, to resign.)

It was in early 1963 that Aliev established contact with Khomeini, through Panahian, a member of the Communist Azerbaijani Party. Shortly after Panahian's arrival in Iraq, he met General Teymour Bakhtiar (cousin of Shahpour Bakhtiar), founder and first chief of the SAVAK. After having been dismissed from his duties, Bakhtiar joined forces with Khomeini. He made the introduction between Khomeini and Panahian, who returned with the ayatollah's writings. These were sent to the Tudeh Party's printing press in Leipzig. Thus the Iranian communists in exile became the first to publish Khomeini's writings. After Bakhtiar was assassinated in Baghdad, Panahian was replaced by the Ayatollah Khoeinha (now Vice-President of the Islamic Republic), who subsequently made several trips to Leipzig in East Germany. A number of Moscow's mullahs (ayatollahs Guilani and Reychahri, the hojatoleslam Mechkini, etc.) have key positions in Khomeini's entourage, while others have appeared in the present government's hierarchy. For example, the hojatoleslam Doai, presently Khomeini's secretary for the publication of the newspaper Ettelaat, once headed the Persian section of Radio-Baghdad (an appointment he received from Andropov). Ali Khamenei, the President of Khomeini's republic, is an alumnus of the Patrice Lumumba University in Moscow. In 1978, the Ayatollah Shariat-Madari spoke out against the infiltration of the ranks of mullahs by "Marxist groups," but in reality, the KGB had been recruiting agents among theological students in Qum and other religious centers for a great many years. Now the Tudeh Party has been once again officially eliminated, its leaders arrested and imprisoned. (None of them has been executed, thanks to the intervention of the "red" mullahs.) However the links with Moscow, through these "red" mullahs and agents in other important posts, have not been broken.

SOVIET ESPIONAGE IN IRAN: In the autumn of 1973 our government arrested two Soviet spies. One was General Ahmad Mogharabi, chief adjunct of the Division of Planning and Logistics in the Imperial Army, who had been in the service of the KGB since 1964. That year, he had been sent to Fort Bragg in the U.S., for specialized training. He was approached by a young woman who showed him incriminating photographs of secret documents he had passed in 1952 (under Mossadegh's government) to a friend in the Tudeh Party. He was told that if he did not cooperate, the photo would be turned over to the SAVAK. "If you work for us," the young woman said, "you will be well compensated. And if your position should become dangerous, we will protect you by sending you to the Soviet Union." For eleven months, the General gave confidential information to his contacts, two Soviet "diplomats," members of the KGB, who were later declared persona non grata and expelled. In December 1977, the General was tried, convicted and executed by firing squad. The second spy was Alinaghi Rabani, a high-ranking government official married to a socially prominent woman. He had been recruited in 1947 in Meshed, by a member of the Tudeh Party, who introduced him to a KGB agent working under cover of the Irano-Soviet Cultural Society. As instructed by his new employers, he moved to Tehran and secured a position in the offices of the President of the Council of Ministers. Rabani was also condemned to death, but escaped execution through the intervention of his wife's powerful relatives. These were only two of many examples of Soviet subversion. In my country there are numerous areas for recruitment, as well as organizations which serve as "fronts" for subversive activity—various cultural societies, the Soviet Hospital of Tehran, the Ispahan Steelworks, the Tass and Novonti agencies, the Soviet Insurance Company, the Soviet Transport Society, Aeroflot, the Soviet Commercial Mission, embassies, consulates, etc. In Iran, we also have a large Armenian community, which the Soviets courted during their occupation of the north during World War I. Some of these Armenians emigrated to Russia. Using bribery and intimidation, Russian agents were often able to recruit the relatives who remained in Iran.

The Soviet presence in Iran began to show itself actively in 1977, with the inauguration of my brother's liberalization policies. Former members of the Tudeh Party began to publish a weekly called "Navid" on the offset press in the Soviet Embassy. During the summer of 1978, "Navid" began publishing supplementary editions for the dissemination of misinformation. When, during the same period, the Tudeh Party in exile joined forces with Khomeini, "Navid" similarly began to support the clerical position. In the fall of 1978, Moscow's hand in the disturbances which were taking place in Tehran became clearer. The Soviet Embassy began importing large consignments of paper in July and October. Heavy purchases of Iranian currency were made by the Soviets on the European market. Increasingly, broadcasts hostile to our regime were beamed from the clandestine radio stations in the name of the Tudeh Party. Suppressed communists resurfaced, well-organized and well-equipped, to participate aggressively in the demonstrations supporting Khomeini. Over the years, liberal western observers criticized my brother for what they saw as his obsession with the Soviet threat, his appetite for sophisticated weaponry. They likened the attitude of the Soviets to the attitude of American policymakers during the 1950s at the height of the cold war. They disparaged his tendency to view discrete events—like the creation of Bangladesh, Soviet friendship treaties with India and Iraq, the fall of the monarchy in Afghanistan—as part of a pincers movement aimed at Iran, with the intent of reaching the Indian Ocean through her.

During the summer and fall of 1978, it seemed to us that these fears were being substantiated. Articles in "Navid" and other Soviet-inspired publications provided an insight into the Iranian communists' attempt to exploit the Islamic fundamentalist movement in Iran for their own purposes. As early as June, 1978, a pamphlet sponsored by "Navid" and titled "The Tudeh Party and the Muslim Movement," advocated an "anti-dictatorial front" in which Khomeini's mullahs would play a vanguard role. It concluded: "We are ready to put at the disposal of our friends from the clergy and other political groups, all our political, propaganda and technical resources for the campaign against the Shah." About this trend, Robert Moss wrote, in his study on *The Campaign to Destabilize the* Shah (November 1978): "This is the most striking evidence that has come to light so far of the Communist stake in the Muslim revolt in Iran. It is not an isolated example. The Tudeh Party's line was clearly established as early as 1973, when it issued, under Soviet guidance, a program entitled: 'The Creation of a Monolithic Front Against the Iranian Regime,' which called for the formation of a broad-based coalition of Communists, Muslims and liberal forces to topple the Shah. The same theme has been rehearsed by Radio-Moscow since 1975 when it replied to a (probably fictitious) letter from anonymous mullahs by suggesting that Marxism and Islam were compatible and would unite to implement a revolutionary program in Iran." Although contacts between the Iranian clergy and Moscow go back for many years, I know it still seems unlikely to some that the USSR would support a fundamentalist movement in the Muslim world. Analysts who subscribe to the so-called "Islamic Map" theory point out that a religious movement of this kind might appeal to the population of the southern republics of the USSR and lead to separatism. They also point to historical precedents; in 1920 Lenin renounced the idea of spreading the revolution to our country because he was afraid that Russian Muslims might defect to Iran. For the same reason, he supported Ataturk, rather than the communists, in Turkey. They also point out that as late as 1946, Stalin abandoned two communist republics in the north of Iran, so as not to create a Muslim bloc that might be difficult or impossible to control. Ours is an area where the Soviets have exercised some caution in implementing their goals. I believe that in the past this was dictated by political considerations and necessities which no longer apply, which invalidates the notion of an "Islamic Card" as a deterrent to the spread of communist objectives. Lenin and after him, Stalin, abandoned the Iranian communists, just as the communists in Germany and in China were abandoned. With the civil war and the paralysis of their economy, the Soviets were in no position to divert their resources to spreading revolution elsewhere. Furthermore, in 1946, with Russia ravaged by war, Stalin was in no position to confront the U.S., a superpower with nuclear weapons who had supported Iran's territorial integrity. Today these considerations no longer apply. And the Soviets no longer have reason to fear the seduction of their own Muslim populations by the existence of an Islamic republic, based on the interpretation of the Koran by the clergy. Today, six years into their own Islamic republic, Iranians have suffered enormously. The quality of life, economically and socially, is so poor that it can have no appeal to others outside. In fact, it has generated among Iranians a widespread repugnance for the concept of Islam as a governing force and generated a backlash which the leftists can turn to their own advantage. Given this situation, the Islamic map is not serious a deterrent to Soviet regional ambitions. On the contrary, it may well be the means by which the leftist extremists can seize power in Iran. Certainly this is the hope of Rajavils Mujahiddin. It may be the way in which Khrushchev's prophecy that Iran would fall, like a piece of rotten fruit into Russians hands, can be realized. It is a tool which the Russians have played against the U.S. in the Gulf area, and it will be used with particular effectiveness in Iran, unless the mullahs are ousted and replaced with a government that can return my country to the twentieth century.

The communist role in the overthrow of the Shah is clear to me, but I must now ask again why it was ignored by the Carter administration, which was so intent on its policy of detente that it ignored the intelligence reports and warning of its own allies. As early as 1978, it is said that the MOSSAD, the Israeli secret service, knew about a Soviet plan to destabilize Iran "in the months to come"—and so reported to Washington. According to the same source (a speech given on May 14, 1979, by Arnaud de Borchgrave to the members of the France-America Society), a European secret service submitted a similar report, with additional details. Yet spokesmen for the Carter administration declared that the Soviet Union was not involved, in spite of growing evidence to the contrary. There was an impressive degree of organization and coordination in the supposedly spontaneous demonstrations that occurred after June 1978, when the leftists joined with Khomeini's followers. Furthermore, our secret police noted (and I'm certain the intelligence service of the U.S. did the same) that it was Soviet-trained Tudeh Party members who organized the shutdown of our oil industry—the first of a series of strikes and demonstrations that shook the country. According to de Borchgrave, western leaders chose to alter or conceal information of this kind, in order to maintain the position that there was no evidence of Soviet involvement—thus to keep detente and SALT negotiations on track. (A similar policy was pursued at the time of the Marxist coup in Afghanistan, and in the period before, when massive Soviet air and infantry concentrations were deliberately played down.)

It is not that I mean to suggest that the Soviets alone were responsible for subversive activities in Iran, but their role in destabilizing Iran was a key one. I do not believe that their original intention was to overthrow my brother. I think their principal concern was the introduction in our country (by the mid-seventies) of highly sophisticated surveillance devices, the stockpiling of huge quantities of arms and my brother's determination to proceed with his ambitious military program. Their original objective, I believe, was to embarrass the Shah and the

United States and to stop the flow of arms and spying devices. In the first months of the Carter administration, they were confronted by human rights protests concerning their own dissidents. They responded by intensifying the campaign against the Shah. And when they saw that many of Carter's aides were eager to oust my brother, they escalated their efforts to destabilize his regime. At that point, my brother was aiding the new republican regime in Afghanistan. His departure would serve the Soviets both in Iran and Afghanistan and strengthen the position of their friends in South Yemen and the Arabian peninsula.

The end result in Iran may not have been what they anticipated. The crushing of the Tudeh Party, the arrest and public display of its leaders, their confession of spying on Muslim behalf, has damaged the Soviet position in Iran. However, as I have pointed out, the lives of these leaders were spared, at a time when no such mercy was shown to others. Furthermore, Moscow has never relied exclusively on the Tudeh Party to carry out its objectives, and I know this to be true now, even within Khomeini's regime.

4: THE UNITED STATES ROLE

THE U.S. ROLE: July 1976. I remember very clearly the period when the U.S. was celebrating its 200th birthday, for it was a time when the campaign against my brother accelerated and grew to unprecedented proportions. Student demonstrations multiplied on college campuses and around our embassies and consulates. American human rights organizations joined the protests and were given extensive press coverage. This was not the first time we had seen student demonstrations against the Shah in the U.S. The first time was in 1959, after Iran signed a contract with Enrico Mattei, head of Ente Nacional Idrocarburi (ENI), an Italian oil company and maverick competitor of the international oil giants. Mattei had agreed to a 75%-25% split of profits, in our favor. At that time our intelligence services reported that "Big Oil" and the CIA were behind the demonstrations against my brother. Relations between the U.S. and Iran were excellent at the time, and the major oil companies were making enormous profits. But we in Iran know that the powerful oil industry has traditionally employed both direct and indirect pressure to protect its interests.

BIG OIL AND IRAN: The development of the oil industry in my country, indeed in the entire Middle East, is marked by intrigues, political and economic upheavals, acts of terrorism and bloody revolutions. In his last book, my brother wrote: "To understand the upheaval in Iran and other parts of the Middle East, one must understand the politics of oil." *(Answer to History, 1980)*. The politics started with the British who had acquired the rights to exploit and sell the oil from our southern fields in 1901. When our oil industry was nationalized in 1951, under Mossadegh's prime ministership, they responded with a number of sanctions, including an embargo on our production. After lengthy negotiations, we were able to reach a basic agreement with a consortium of the world's eight largest oil companies. Our National Iranian Oil Company, as owner, employed the consortium as its contract agent for the operation and sale of oil. The agreement was to remain in effect for 25 years (with an option for three five-year extensions) and gave us 50% of the profits. The Shah's objective was complete Iranian control over our oil resources (of course, the objective of the oil companies was to avert or postpone this event and to maximize their gains whenever historical necessity dictated renegotiation). In 1957, he was able to reduce the consortium's power by having the parliament adopt the Iran Petroleum Act, which allowed more foreign companies into the country and extended the activities of the NIOC. He signed a contract with Matteis ENI and later, another with Pan American Oil Company. In 1958, he attempted to modify the agreement with the consortium, so that NIOC would assure full management responsibility. The negotiations, which took 15 years, were concluded on July 31, 1973. The consortium became, in effect, a simple buyer of our crude.

From the time of my brother's first moves towards independence in 1957, we saw a series of events which certainly make sense in the light of our "oil connection." The first among these was Matteis death in a plane crash, termed an accident due to "lack of visibility." This was followed by a systematic media campaign of denigration against my brother and his government. A picture of the Shah as "despot" began to be widely circulated. During the past thirty years or so I have spent a great deal of time in the west, and I see that cultural prejudices on both sides unfortunately make this kind of distortion and cari-caturing very easy (for example, just as the Middle East's leaders are often portrayed here as dark and sinister individuals with dark and sinister designs, America has often been portrayed, as it is now in Iran, as an unscrupulous and hungry "satan," ready to exploit and manipulate the less fortunate countries of the world.) During this early period, professional agitators operat-ing through "student" organizations first appeared. The campaign reached a peak in 1961 and then died out. In 1973, the OPEC ministers met in Tehran, in response to a request from my brother. They decided to raise the price of oil from 5.032 dollars to 11.651 dollars a barrel. International pressure groups immediately responded with another mass media campaign, in which he was accused of attempting the disintegration of the west's economies. Of course it would have been unprofitable to add the oil—the principal and irreplaceable resource in our part of the world which had been pitifully underpriced for a great many years. As one of the first regional leaders to recog-nize and redress the imbalance, my brother found himself on the cover of *Time* magazine (November 4, 1974), with the cap-tion: "The Emperor of Oil." Far from being the "price hawk" depicted in the West, he was consistently a reasonable and prac-tical voice among our OPEC partners, counseling moderation, with an eye towards orderly and rational growth. After 1975, he repeatedly attempted to keep oil prices in check. In 1977, for example, he complied with a western request to freeze prices. In 1978, Cyrus Vance and his British counterpart, David Owen, approached my brother and asked him to hold the line. He agreed—but the campaign continued.

Suddenly, the demonstrations, which had been small and sporadic until 1977, grew larger and more constant. The pre-sentation of my brother as the "real" hawk in OPEC, as the single figure most responsible for soaring oil prices became a popular one. It was an effective piece of symbolism for focusing public anger and blame (certainly more functional than publishing the balance sheets of the oil companies, which were still quite healthy) for a host of problems. Another effective means for focusing pressure on my brother was the human rights issue, which served the oil companies as well as it did the Soviet Union and the Iranian opposition. During the American primaries and the presidential campaign, candidate Jimmy Carter focused heavily on the human rights issue. Iran was singled out as a major offender—certainly there were political prisoners in Iran, and cases of torture, as reported by Amnesty International. Within our country, a number of people were accused of corruption. Given the history of our region, these problems were not particular to my country, and in fact, they are found to some extent in virtually all our neighboring countries. Yet Iran was singled out. Our secret police, the SAVAK (which also have their counterpart among our neighbors) was accused of "coercive methods" and portrayed as an all-powerful, ubiquitous extension of the Shah's policy (though, as history has demonstrated, it was riddled with the same kind of factionalism and intrigue so common in the Middle East). As Professor George Lenczowski wrote, after the revolution:

"On a comparative scale, they (corruption and coercion) did not appear any more severe than in the adjoining countries, whether the oil-rich Arab monarchies or the one-party military dictatorship. In fact, secret police supervision, jailing on mere suspicion, long imprisonment without a court sentence, and execution after summary trials—acts that sharply contrasted with the due process of law in the West—were not uncommon in both categories of states.

"Moreover, certain radical dictatorships were prone to resort to individual assassinations of their political enemies and those accused of deviation from the official party line. In short coercion in these countries has often exceeded in crude brutality the measures applied by the Iranian security organs, and yet it seldom if ever led to massive revolutionary protests. Interestingly enough, however, western news media seemed to concentrate with an almost sadistic persistence on these features of the Iranian regime." (*Foreign Affairs, Spring 1979, "The Arc of Crisis"*).

PRESIDENT KENNEDY AND IRAN: Direct intervention in the affairs of Iran did not, of course, begin with Jimmy Carter. When I was in New York for the autumn (1976) session of the UN, I noted with mounting apprehension the intensification of attacks on my brother throughout the Carter-Ford campaign. I recalled the problems which had marred relations between our two countries during the Kennedy administration. In those days Third World countries were just beginning to emerge as independent entities on the world political scene. The Democrats hailed the decolonization trend, though they were reluctant to pursue the Eisenhower policy of selling arms and giving aid to what they characterized as "right wing dictatorships." Their foreign policy in our part of the world appeared to have the following direction: The U.S. should move more quickly than the U.S.S.R. in extending aid to the newly independent countries; support should be given to groups representing real national values and seeking national self-determination; the U.S. should avoid helping reactionary and unpopular regimes to keep themselves in power. Based on this position, the Kennedy administration often took an "interventionist" stance in the internal affairs of small countries. In his last book, my brother noted one instance of this intervention in our country:

"The U.S. wanted him (Prime Minister Emami) out and its own man in as Prime Minister. This man was Ali Amini, and in time the pressure became too strong for me to resist, especially after John Kennedy was elected President. John F. Kennedy was never against me. I remember him as a friend, although we had little direct contact. I remember so well my first meetings with the Kennedys at the White House: Jacqueline Kennedy spoke of Amini's wonderfully flashing eyes and how much she hoped I would name him Prime Minister. Eventually I gave Amini the job. There have been rumors that Kennedy offered me a 35 million dollar aid package as an inducement. These rumors are totally unfounded, for it was Amini who obtained this money from the U.S. after he became prime minister. But he mismanaged affairs so badly that he was soon asking the Americans for another 60 million dollars, which was refused."

I remember that the Kennedy administration later pressured the Shah again into appointing another "liberal" prime minister: Ali Mansour, who was assassinated in 1965. These experiences left my brother wondering about American understanding of our political realities. American's part in the overthrow and death of Ngo Dinh Diem in 1963 raised his doubts about the reliability of an American alliance. "Poor Diem," he said to me. "The Americans have abandoned an ally, one who served as a deterrent against communist expansion, and they have opened a Pandoras box." This was the first time I had heard him express such doubts. "They followed the fashion of the day in their foreign policies," he continued, "without considering the impact of new ideas and new policies on people and countries unlike their own. I wish they would heed Toynbee's observation that all people are not contemporary, though we do live on the same planet. The world isn't a laboratory," he said impatiently. "Nor are the people of the world guinea pigs to shape according to their ideas and images."

In the years to come, I would often recall those words, as I heard my brother and my country being attacked for failing to conform to western liberal ideals (ironically, we are now seeing the same kind of prejudice in the Iran of Khomeini). About this period of U.S.-Iranian relations, American journalist Richard Sale observed: "Because of the Soviet threat, U.S. policymakers felt it was crucial that Iran be politically stable; this required a genuinely popular political leadership. There was, they said, a great difference between subduing a multitude and ruling a society. According to the Americans, the only Iranian leader with the required political abilities was Ali Amini, who had brilliantly represented Iran at the International Oil Consortium talks in

1954. 'We created Amini for the role,' said a State Department official of the 1960s The difficulty was that the plan failed."[18] *(The Washington Quarterly*, Autumn 1980, "Carter and Iran: From Idealism to Disaster.") In 1977 the Carter administration exerted the same kind of pressure and insisted on an immediate liberalization of political life in Iran. Although my brother had similar goals in mind, he understood, as the Americans did not, that liberalization was not the answer to all of Iran's problems, that insistence on the application of western values to eastern problems could prove disastrous. Adda Bozeman, Professor Emeritus of International Affairs at Sarah Lawrence College, states the problem: "Heedless of the threats that had been accumulating steadily on Iran's northern and eastern frontiers—which, lest we forget, had been recognized also as the boundaries of our own security zone—and unconcerned about the nature of Iran's Islamic and pre-Islamic orientations towards the rights and obligations of citizens, we chose to indict the Teheran government publicly, time and time again, for violating norms and values unique to Western civilizations.[19] (in ORBIS, a journal of world affairs, Summer 1979). This time the move was accompanied by a powerful media campaign generated by the communists, who found in the policies of the new American government, opportunities for their own advancement, which they successfully exploited in Iran, as well as in Africa and Latin America. President Carter, not unlike John Kennedy, advocated negotiations with the Soviets and the propagation and implementation of human rights policies, according to western standards. And although the new foreign policy trends proved disastrous (not only in Iran, but in Nicaragua, in Afghanistan, etc.), the American interests they meant to serve remained the same as they had been for all American administrations since World War II.

U.S. INTEREST IN IRAN: The refusal of the Soviets to evacuate Northern Iran after the war pushed us towards the U.S., which was emerging on the postwar scene as the foremost "superpower." The occupation of our country since 1941 by the

Russians and the British had weakened the central government and allowed a revival of feudalism. The tribal leaders and the big landowners were once again independently ruling their own territories, while the clergy had resumed its control of the judicial and educational system. Superseding these were the foreign occupiers, who virtually dominated all aspects of our daily life. The movement toward modernization and unification of the bureaucracy, begun by my father Reza Shah, had fallen apart. The 1907 agreement, dividing Iran into spheres of influence, seemed once more to be operational.

We Iranians did not feel like allies (though we had served as Russia's supply line during the war), but more like a conquered people. This was the disheartening and demoralizing situation which my brother, who was then a young man in his 20s, had inherited. Instinctively, he turned to President Roosevelt, to exert some pressure on the other two allies. By January 1942, a treaty was signed, guaranteeing our independence and our territorial integrity. The U.S., the British and the Soviets agreed to withdraw their armies not later than six months after the war's end. Iran was very much in need of economic and military assistance. As our pre-war allies, the European countries, were themselves in the grip of formidable difficulties, we turned to the U.S., and since that time, a special relationship developed between our two countries, one which endured through each American election, with various modifications and reshapings. By the time Jimmy Carter was in the White House, a broad bipartisan consensus existed in Congress, regarding the following points:

- Deterrence of Soviet penetration in the region (Iran's economic dependence on the U.S. ended, and we were able to pay for our arms purchases. By 1977, Iran was a regional power, helping maintain stability in the Persian Gulf region).
- The flow of oil to the West and to Japan.
- Maintenance of beneficial economic and commercial relations (by the seventies, the U.S. was the largest supplier of

civilian and military goods in Iran. The sudden rupture of these exchanges in 1979 created an immediate deficit in trade balance of the U.S.).

It was in the process of implementing "new" policies in our region, that the U.S. lost these advantages. In retrospect, I must ask "why?" since the changes were instituted at a time when relations between our two countries seemed excellent to American analysts. It is true that there were areas of concern on both sides. U.S. analysts signaled that Iran was becoming increasingly "independent and assertive" (I find this to be a curious paradox in a country which energetically deplores the idea of "puppet" governments). As I have mentioned, Americans blamed my brother for the rise in oil prices. America was concerned over my country's rapidly developing ties with Arab countries, particularly with such states as Iraq and Syria. These ties, in the view of some Americans, increased Israel's isolation. On our side, there were, as I have mentioned, misgivings over the assassination of Diem during the Kennedy presidency, CIA involvement in anti-Iranian demonstrations, and the use of the human rights issue as an instrument of foreign policy. In 1975, once again, the abandonment of south Vietnam and its subsequent invasion by the north, raised questions about the reliability of American support. The hospitable climate in the U.S. towards dissident factions was also a matter of reflection for my brother. Later, he worried about American indecision regarding the "Horn of Africa" and the declarations of Andrew Young on the "stabilizing effect" of Cuban troops in Ethiopia, Angola, and Mozambique. The turnabout in American security arrangements with Taiwan was another source of concern. The growing congressional furor over Iranian arms purchases, along with the flow of commentaries on human rights issued from the State Department raised the important question: Was the American government trying to embarrass and undermine the Shah? The bilateral security and cooperation treaty, which both our countries signed in 1959, was still in effect, but the signals from America, both official and unofficial, were becoming increasingly ambiguous and ambivalent.

ENTERS CARTER: For us in Iran—and particularly for us in the Royal Family—the first omen of things to come was a relatively small matter: The Shah's cable of congratulations to the President-elect remained unanswered for more than a month. White House aides later accounted for the lapse as "sloppy staff work." But in Iran, rumors circulated, fanned by the opposition, that this incident signaled an abandonment of the Shah by the U.S. Even those who were close to the Shah were worried. Such a reaction might appear extreme to Americans. But Iranian psychology is quite different, and the Iranian mentality tends to seek clues to future developments in small and seemingly insignificant details, particularly when those details involve foreign powers (which is why, incidentally, the mere fact that the Americans entered into discussions with Khomeini's people was enough to signal that he would be the next ruler of Iran). As the new president prepared to take office, a new group of policy makers were assigned to key posts in the White House and in other agencies related to the shaping of foreign policy. All these highly influential advisers, liberal in persuasion, appeared to share what columnist Meg Greenfield called the "Populist Perception," namely that any foreign leader who is friendly to the U.S. is probably of no value as a friend, whereas any leftist leader may be assumed to enjoy the support of his people. One of the draftsmen of Carter's foreign policy put this idea in somewhat cruder terms when he remarked: "We finally decided we didn't have to support every son of a bitch around the world just because he was our son of a bitch."[20]

From my point of view, the makeup of the group of men who would shape American policy in Iran was disheartening. A number of key people were personally prejudiced against my brother, favoring a fundamental change in U.S.-Iranian relations, as well as a change of government in Tehran. And though there were differences, the Carter people appeared united by a common "revulsion" towards the Shah's rule, which they considered as heavily dependent on the "stick" of security forces and the "carrot" of vast sums of money. It was these members of the administration who played a dominant role in shaping policies towards Iran—by accident, rather than by design, it would seem, for I'm certain no administration would be willing to acknowledge responsibility for seating Khomeini on the Peacock Throne. Later, Secretary of State Vance would admit that "he paid insufficient attention to the mounting Iranian crisis because he was distracted by arms limitation talks with the Soviet Union and the Camp David Middle-East negotiations."[21] The same state of affairs appeared to exist in the National Security Council, leaving many important questions to second-rank officials—a trademark of the Carter administration. Important issues concerning the fate of my country and my brother were left to the following men:

David Aaron: Deputy Assistant to the President for National Security Affairs. He had previously been Senator Mondale's national security adviser and had close contacts with the Iranian opposition in the U.S.

Warren Christopher: Undersecretary of State, he had served under George Ball (when he was Under secretary of State), who was a critic of the Shah during the Kennedy administration. According to IER, he sent Ramsey Clark to make contact with Khomeini in February, 1979.

Pat Derrian: Director of the Human Rights Bureau of the State Department. According to R. Sale, her list concerning Iran was basic: the Shah was to release all political prisoners, hold free elections, prosecute the most corrupt members of the regime- and exile me! John D. Stempel, director of the State Department Operations Center, writes that she "welcomed the overthrow of the Shah. With her ... friends, she considered the embassy office in Tehran as filled with hopelessly 'retrogressive fascists,' because they supported the Shah."[22]

Richard Holbrooke: Assistant Secretary of State for East Asian and Pacific Affairs. His expressed opinion of my country: "Iran is the worst country I have ever been in."[23]

Robert Hunter: A member of the National Security Council, a friend of D. Aaron and W.J. Miller. He was Edward Kennedy's top foreign policy aide and since the early 1970s a virulent critic of the Shah.

William J. Miller: Head of the staff of the Senate Select Committee on Intelligence. He had served five years in Iran and was very critical of the Shah. Appointed head of the Iran desk of the State Department in the early Nixon years, he was soon removed because of his constant criticism of the administration's Iranian policy. He later played a key role in establishing contact between Henry Precht and a Khomeini adviser at Georgetown University.

Walter F. Mondale: Vice President and, according to Richard Sale, considered a step above Brzezinski, the National Security Adviser to the President.

Henry Precht: Head of the State Department's Iran Desk, who had served in Iran. He did not hide his personal dislike of the Shah and maintained close contact with Mehdi Haeri (an Islamic scholar at Georgetown University), whose father had been one of Khomeini's teachers in Qum. Secret documents published after the "student" takeover of the American Embassy revealed that Precht had established contact with Khomeini through Ibrahim Yazdi—and that both sides agreed "that neither of us would acknowledge that there had been any official contact between Khomeini and that U.S. Government." Later, a State Department official would say of him: "Precht was a pillar. He was anti-military and anti-Shah and he really stood firm."

William Quandt: Member of the National Security Council. He had already been in the NSC in the early '70s. He was an acerbic critic of the Shah and of the previous administration's policies in Iran.[24]

I found it remarkable that from the early days of the Carter government, Iran's fate was left in the hands of these aides of the second rank, who were personally antagonistic to the Shah and his regime. As Richard Sale wrote: "The NSC group working up Iran assessments consisted of Aaron, Jessica Tuchman of the Global Issues Office, William B. Quandt and Navy Captain

Gary G. Sick, who in 1976 had been country director for Persian Gulf Sheikdoms and the Indian Ocean Area at the Defense Department and who presently handles Iran. Informal contributions were made by Robert E. Hunter. Said an insider: 'He had a lot to say at the meetings, and he may have written a memo or two.' It was left to Sick to draft any formal memoranda or papers required. According to a State Department official among the group, there were always those who saw the Shah as being the problem and felt his survival was not desired. What was desired was an orderly transition." According to an administration critic, the group was watched closely by some who were privately convinced that by March, 1977 "they had evolved a policy that was trendy and very anti-Shah. Since the Shah was pro-Israel and pro-U.S., a tyrant who was building up military forces by using an anti-Soviet rationale, he had to be removed." When asked if the Aaron group had actually called for my brother's ouster, a high level State Department official replied: "There were people in State, one on the NSC and one in the U.S. Embassy in Tehran who saw the Shah as being part of the problem; therefore the Shah's departure became an option under serious discussion. This is not the same as calling for an ouster, yet many observers have come to recognize that Carter's foreign policy themes contributed to the Shah's fall."[25] As for the experts and other unofficial advisers who counseled the administration, they were in the main opposed to the Shah's regime and, in some cases, had assisted the opposition.

U.S. RESPONSIBILITY: The presence of such a team of inside and outside Iran "experts" was a gift to the opposition. Never before had there been so many sympathizers in an American administration. Without delay, they established contacts with the new administration in Washington and the American Embassy in Tehran. John Stempel, who arrived in Tehran in July 1975, wrote: "First as political officer, then as deputy chief of the political section, and finally as acting chief of the section, I would come to know personally many of the Iranians, particularly among the opposition, who would play important roles in the revolutionary drama."[26] Documents published by the "students" show that the dissidents had close contact with American diplomats between 1976–78, that there was an ongoing exchange of advice between them. In January 1977, they were told that the Carter administration strongly supported human rights abroad and that Iran was no exception. Encouraged by this advice (and reading into it a "green light," rather than a simple endorsement of their right to free expression, the opposition surfaced and reconstituted their parties and groups. The National Front (Karim Sanjabi), the Liberation Movement (Mehdi Bazargan), the Writer's Syndicate (Ali Asghar Haj Sayid Javadi), the Lawyer's Guild (Hedayatollah matinDaf tary) and the Radical movement (Rahmatollah Moghadam-Maraghei) reformed and together organized a Committee for Human Rights. They published and distributed leaflets attacking the Shah's government. They compiled a document on alleged human rights violations and sent a copy to President Carter. The clergy were also aware of the shift in American position. Prominent mullahs began to deliver political sermons in their mosques. In the U.S., Ibrahim Yazdi, now an American citizen, rekindled his Muslim Students Association and flew to Najaf to discuss with Khomeini the advantages that might by gained from the anti-Shah feelings within the administration.

It was at this time that Anthony Parsons, Britain's last ambassador to our court, talked openly about the impact of Carter's position on my brother's position: "President Carter's ingenuous public espousal of the cause of human rights in Third World Countries, including Iran ... did nothing to allay the Shah's fears. A period of uncertainty in Iran-American relations ensued. Needless to say the reactions of the Shah's opponents, particularly the large and vociferous student associations in the U.S. and the political leaders in Tehran (whose fortunes had briefly prospered in President Kennedy's day) were precisely the reverse. They took comfort and courage from what they rightly detected as a potential weakening of the absolute support which their enemy had received from Washington for so many years."[27] The Shah had already relaxed controls over the press and public assembly, and SAVAK had been ordered to refrain from interfering, as long as the activity of the opposition was not geared for violent uprising. However, the stance of the American administration encouraged the dissidents to press for further concessions.

This was a time of isolation and siege for my brother. Added to the steady pressures from the Soviets (through their powerful propaganda machinery and the activities of the Tudeh leftists), the Qaddafi-supported, anti-Iranian activity in Europe, he was now confronted with pressure from an ally of 37 years standing, an administration dominated by individuals personally antagonistic to him and who was encouraging, aiding and advising those who would overthrow his government.

As I have previously mentioned, the terrorism which had shaken the streets of our major cities stopped early in 1977. This sudden shift worried by brother. "This is not a fortuitous accident," he told me in March. "This is only a change in tactics. Something is going to happen … time is running short. I will have to speed up the democratization of our society." This was a crucial error on my brother's part. Indeed something did happen. The secular opposition joined with the mullahs and the merchants of the Bazaar and presented one series of demands after another. They published slogans for authentic parliamentary democracy—and I must make it clear that these were for western consumption (as events have certainly proved). Any literal implementation of these demands would have resulted in a caricature of western democracy, as has happened in other Third World countries—and indeed in Iran, in the past. The responsibility of the Carter administration in weakening and undermining a friendly government was a crucial one. Even without attributing personal prejudice and design to its members (which certainly did exist in some cases), I can say that this intervention and interference was carried out without a knowledgeable assessment of the impact they would have on either the Iranian people—or on the vital interests of the U.S. Sir Anthony Parsons makes these observations:

"I believe it to be the case that if the Shah had not 'liberalized' at the end of 1976, he would still be on the throne, or rather his son would if the Shah had died in the meantime of cancer. It was the gradual and increasingly uncontrollable release of opposition which followed the liberalization that enabled the disparate forces to create the momentum, which, when they combined, eventually proved irresistible. If therefore … the Shah liberalized under pressure from the United States government, it can be argued that this was an error in judgment."[28] Paul Nitze, a Carter administration official, puts the idea simply: "There was no conspiracy to oust the Shah. But on the other hand, anyone knew that if you asked him to liberalize, you'd ruin him" (cited by Richard Sale, *The Washington Quarterly*). In yet another assessment, Professor Bozeman writes: "The Carter administration's Iranian disposition (it cannot be called a policy) was ambivalent to say the least. On the one hand, there certainly was the realization that a pro-American, pro-Western Iran, was the capstone of our strategic design in the Middle-East and, therefore, a vital link in the chain of our worldwide security arrangements. On the other hand, one finds what one can only be described as an obstinate, even irrational insistence to embarrass the one internationally prestigious ally we had in the region, and in the measure that we accomplished this, of course, our own strategic design was invalidated."[29]

Time and time again I have asked myself how a country like the United States could dispose of a friendly government so cavalierly—and so shortsightedly. Two more puzzle pieces contribute to an answer of sorts. One is supplied by Ibrahim Yazdi, an American citizen of Iranian origins who was one of Khomeini's closest associates (who fell from power after documents seized by Iranian students brought to light his contract with American diplomats and CIA operatives). In a book published in Farsi and titled *Last Moves in the Last Days*, he says that the Americans knew of my brother's cancer and saw this as another reason for removing him. Yazdi adds that after Carter's election, the "liberal" elements in the Democratic party became stronger than the conservative and the military. They argued, he said, that the sudden death of the Shah would lead to uncertainty and that an orderly transition was in American's best interests. Their conclusion, one which they pressed, was that a change of regime was desirable. The other puzzle piece has to do with the west's tendency to cling to the "Islamic card" as a weapon against the spread of communism.

THE ISLAMIC CARD: This is another flawed idea, one which has been advocated by scholars as well as policy makers, namely that the so-called "Islamic card" is an effective bulwark against Soviet expansion. The idea is an old one. It has its roots in the end of the 19th century in Britain, following the brief adventure of the Mahdi who took Khartoum and expelled the English for a short time from the Sudan. There were those politicians and intelligence operatives who deemed it useful to manipulate the incipient Muslim Brotherhood and to use it to further British interests against the Ottoman Empire. The origins of this underground movement can be traced back to Jamaladin Afghani, an Islamic reformer, and to various splinter groups who attempted to revive the idea of "jihad" or "holy war." The Islamic Brotherhood (Ikhwan) was formally and openly constituted in Egypt in 1928, by Hassan al Banna, the first "Imam" of the organization. In 1954, the British and Israelis used it against Colonel Nasser, who was moving towards nationalization of the Suez Canal Company. Nasser responded by publicly exposing the Ikhwan's links to MOSSAD (Israeli intelligence). On October 26, 1954, as Nasser was addressing a huge crowd, a Brotherhood terrorist fired six shots at him. Mass arrests and executions quickly followed, and the movement went underground again. The Brotherhood relocated in London, Geneva, and, under a number of guises, in other western countries, including the U.S. Today the thinking behind the Islamic card is this: That the Muslim countries, particularly those located near the southern borders of the USSR, can be used as a shield against the southward spread of communism. Furthermore, it is hoped that "Islamic fever" might spill over into the Muslim republics of the Soviet Union and cause disruption (as it is hoped that Catholicism in eastern Europe will do). Partisans of this idea argue that it is Islamic fervor which animates the fighting in Afghanistan, against the Soviet invasion. William Sullivan, Carter's ambassador to Tehran was an advocate of the "Islamic belt" policy. In an article he wrote in 1982, he suggested that:

> "The regime of Saddam Hussein in Iraq faces likely collapse in 1983 … For all practical purposes, Iraq already has lost the war with Iran …
>
> "Should a Shi'ite regime come to power in Baghdad, this would constitute an enormous success for Khomeini. Far more important, however, it would signal the beginning of a new political force in the region: a 'northern tier' of anti-Sunni Muslim states in the Middle East. This 'northern tier' would consist of a configuration of allies centered on Iran, Iraq and Syria …
>
> "This grouping would be predictably anti-Soviet and probably would do as much to seal off the area against Soviet penetration as the American Rapid Deployment Force …
>
> "In short, the collapse of Saddam Hussein and the establishment of an anti-Sunni belt in the Middle East could make 1983 a milestone in that troubled part of the world. It might mark a halt to any serious Soviet penetration of the area."[30]

There were similar sentiments expressed after the taking of the U.S. Embassy by Jody Powell, Carter's press secretary, when he said he welcomed the resurgent force of Islam in Iran (cited by R. Dreyfus, in Hostage to Khomeini, 1980).[31] Advocates of this Islamic strategy have ignored a number of factors. Soviet Muslims would not find a Khomeini-type regime appealing, not only because they are in the majority Sunnis, but because the way of life it presents is infinitely less attractive than what they enjoy under the Soviets. In fact, the reverse is true: the anachronistic, oppressive, and economically crippled society under the Islamic fundamentalists is far more likely to provide a hospitable climate for communist gains. Furthermore, the religious leaders of today are far more sophisticated, far more aware of their political leverage than they were in the past. They are far more interested in furthering their own political ends than in serving the west. In fact, these days, when I hear arguments by those who believe that Islam will serve the cause of the west, I am reminded of those western politicians who once believed that Nazism would stem the spread of communism.

CARTER'S LEGACY: I have certainly made no secret of my opinion of this last Democratic President, and it is not one that I hold alone. As the Carter-Vance-Brzezinski foreign policy unfolded, some European analysts went so far as to say that "Carter was endangering the whole world."[32] In November, 1979, J.B. Connaly said to a French journalist: "Mr. Carter est le digne heritier de Neville Chamberlain."[33] One year into the Carter administration, after the President was accused of displaying weakness in various parts of the world, Cyrus Vance made a speech, presumably explaining the basic foreign policy ideas of the new administration. At a meeting of the American Association of Community and Junior Colleges in Chicago, he asserted that the U.S. required a "new kind of diplomacy" to deal with what he called the "deep and rapid change" taking place in a world no longer dominated by traditional power centers. "Most Americans," he added, "now recognize that we alone cannot dictate events. This recognition is not a sign of American's decline. It is a sign of growing American maturity in a complex world."[34] In the meantime, the Soviet Union invaded Afghanistan, then Cuban troops intervened with Andrew Young's blessings, in Ethiopia, Angola and Mozambique. In Somalia, the administration encouraged the president to resist Ethiopia's Marxist regime—but later failed to support him. In Chad, Vice President Mondale promised Hicene Habre arms—but did not deliver on his promises (Washington tried to induce my brother to supply the arms).

And, then, back home in Iran, America lost its credibility as an ally. As she handed over my country to the mullahs, her diplomats were held hostage, her Embassy occupied, for 14 months. Iran's refugees were treated as undesirables, and in his last days, my brother was denied the medical treatment and the asylum that might have prolonged his life, or at the very least, enabled him to die in peace and dignity. He was treated like a homeless alien, while the Carter administration demonstrated its weakness and inadequacy in the face of Khomeini's blatant criminality. I think Jeanne Kirkpatrick, President Reagan's former ambassador to the United Nations, sums up the failure of Carter's foreign policy quite well:

"In Iran and Nicaragua the Carter administration and the State Department withheld economic aid, weapons, ammunition and moral support and urged the departure of the Shah and Somoza because the administration had a theory that these acts would promote human rights and build democracy in those countries. It is not necessary to believe that the United States 'lost' Iran and Nicaragua to understand that our policies failed to produce the expected consequences. Policy makers acted on the belief, widely held in enlightened circles, that there existed in Iran and Nicaragua moderate democratic groups which represented a progressive alternative to traditional and revolutionary extremes, and that the moderate groups had a good chance of achieving power. Get rid of rightist dictators, support the democratic Left, promote reform, preempt the radicals, build democracy and development: Thus went the theory that gave us the Ayatollah Khomeini and the Ortega brothers. The ayatollah's policies mocked Western expectations that this anti-American holy man was some kind of (moderate) saint, as Nicaragua's continuing militarization, Cubanization and repression mock the expectations of the FSLN's democratic supporters. Once again, good intentions and a mistaken theory produced results as destructive as they were unintended."

"Ideas have consequences, bad ideas have bad consequences."[35]

What I ask now, as I have asked so many times in past years, is who will answer for the consequences of these bad ideas— for American's insistence that Iran instantly give birth to a democratic civilian government (in American's image), though there was nothing in our history (or that of our neighbors) that would support such a creation?

THE WASHINGTON CONSPIRACY: Washington, Fall 1977. A short time after I flew to New York for the annual session of the UN, my brother made a state visit to Washington in the hope of clarifying and reinforcing his relationship with the U.S. government. His visit was, of course, awaited both by pro-Shah resident Iranians and by the forces of opposition. On the day of his arrival at the White House, a crowd of several thousand resident Iranians gathered on the South Ellipse carrying banners that said "Welcome Shah." A much smaller group, several hundred at most, assembled in Lafayette Park, on the other side of the Executive Mansion. They wore paper-bag masks and carried placards: "Masks Protect Us From SAVAK." They claimed to be Iranian students. When the Shah arrived for the welcoming ceremonies, the "student" demonstrators charged the peaceful assembly of supporters; they were swinging placard handles and staves studded with nails. The police, unprepared for violence, used tear gas to restore order, but hundreds of unarmed well-wishers were injured in the melee. Characteristically, the media, which by then had lost or abandoned its objectivity where my brother was concerned, weighted its reports in curious fashion. The numbers were reversed, and it was stated that thousands of Iranian demonstrators had filled Lafayette Park in order to face several hundred pro-Shah people. Little notice was taken of the violent intent of the demonstrators, or of the weapons they carried. One newspaper asked: "Who paid for the Shah's supporters to come to Washington?" Another reported that our embassy had paid all expenses and given each supporter a hundred dollar bill. Not one newspaper or broadcaster raised questions as to the opposition's source of support. A cursory police investigation revealed that most of the "students" were not, in fact, Iranians, but young Americans, Puerto Ricans, Arabs, etc.—whose masks served to hide their origins, rather than their identities. Our secret service learned that funds for the organization of this demonstration had been sent from Europe and Libya, through a dummy Foundation set up in New York and nearby cities. Plane tickets had been furnished to those who lived in Los Angeles and other distant areas. None of this was reported in the press, which carried new attacks on the Shah, and published, once again, the figure of 100,000 political prisoners (a figure which had already been disputed by Amnesty International and other groups). Talks between President Carter and my brother were amicable, and confirmed my brother's opinion that there would be no changes in U.S. foreign policy. He continued to hold this view much too long in my opinion, and even in the face of growing evidence to the contrary.

I had begun to bring up my doubts with him the year before, when I told him of my concern that a number of the President's people were personally opposed to him. He told me not to worry, that the U.S. had too much at stake in the Gulf area to allow any hostile developments there. He reminded me that U.S. foreign policy was bipartisan and could not change overnight. During the Washington visit, Carter praised my brother's policies and encouraged him to continue in the same path. This show of public support puzzled the incipient opposition in Iran. Some of its leaders raised questions with their contacts in the U.S. One of these leaders (who fled from Iran and is now living in hiding in Europe) has told me that his American contacts advised him to disregard official statements in support of the Shah, to pursue and expand opposition activity. Up until the end of 1977 this activity was relatively peaceful, but by early 1978 there were some dramatic changes.

My father, Reza Shah Pahlavi, architect of modern Iran.

Up until the early thirties Iranian women had to be veiled.
My father, Reza Pahlavi, proclaimed their freedom and had
women unveiled. I am seen here together with my sister,
Princess Shams, following my mother on the first day of this
occasion which marked freedom for Iranian women.

My brother the Shah of Iran, dies in lonely exile. He was avoided by government leaders who once flocked to Iran and lined up to see him. This is a reminder of the fragility of friendship in affairs of state.

Princess Ashraf Pahlavi walking amongst Iranian tribal women in a distant Persian village.

5: PLOTS, SCHEMES AND MACHINATIONS

REACTIONS TO VIOLENCE: On January 7, 1978, the first riots erupted, and for the first time, the clergy surfaced as a major source of agitation. Demonstrators surged through the streets of the holy city of Qum. According to our intelligence sources, the demonstrators now included communist and foreign elements, as well as Iranians trained in Palestinian camps. U.S. intelligence knew of the ties between the opposition and the Soviets and the PLO. As Michael Ledeen and William Lewis have written: "It was known that many Palestinians—and particularly those involved in the radical Popular Front for the Liberation of Palestine—have been trained in terrorist camps within the Soviet Union. Yet American policy in the Middle East was moving in the direction of greater dialogue with the PLO and with its titular chief, Yassir Arafat. So when the Americans unearthed evidence that Iranians were receiving paramilitary training from elements of the PLO, this was not taken to be in and of itself alarming news."[36]

I remember that a few days after the Qum riots, 30,000 paraded through the holy city, in support of the Shah. But there had been six casualties in the riots, giving the mullahs their first "martyrs"—the means for using traditional Shi'ite rituals (those attending death and bereavement) as a powerful propaganda tool for inciting and manipulating the masses. (According to tradition, the family and friends of the deceased gather at the tomb forty days after the death.) On February 18, 1978, demonstrations were set up in Tabriz. These turned into riots claiming several more lives. A few weeks later, a crowd of 300,000 demonstrated in Tabriz on behalf of the Shah. But the world press, which had carried the news of the anti-Shah riots, made no mention of this.

The renewal of violence, following a year of calm, was ominous. In April of 1978, I visited my brother at the Niavaran Palace and shared my concern. His response was that this was the price of liberalization and democratization. "I've been advised to allow the police to intervene," he said. "But I am a King and not a despot. If we are to have a more democratic government, the people must be able to assess the realities of their situation. I have tried to improve their standard of living ... I cannot order the police to fire on crowds." His conviction eased some of my anxieties, but what he said next astonished me. "I want you to carry out a goodwill mission to China and Brazil. You must accept the invitations you have received from those countries."

"Don't you think it would be better if I canceled those trips, under the present circumstances?" I asked.

"On the contrary. I have been scheduled to visit East Germany in September, and I plan to do so. It is very important to maintain our relations with other nations."

Though not without doubts, I made these trips. I suspected that there were those in our government who, as in the past, preferred to separate me from my brother—and that they had successfully persuaded him to send me away. As always, I followed the events at home. On June 6, 1978, General Nematollah Nassiri, the head of SAVAK, resigned. As history has demonstrated, this organization had ceased to serve the government and had, in fact, become a liability. Yet as history has also shown, Nassiri's ouster was seen by the opposition, not as a gesture of conciliation (which is not what the opposition was after), but rather as another green light from Washington. Later, when Henry Precht was asked if Iranian intelligence officials like

Hossein Fardust, head of the Imperial Inspectorate, were responsible for Nassirils resignation, he answered: "On the contrary, I think America had a lot to do with it."[37]

In September of 1978, I went to New York, as I did every year, to preside over our delegation to the General Assembly of the UN. The weeks that followed were a nightmare. Under pressure from the U.S., my brother opened the doors of our prisons, and the character of the demonstrations changed once again. While one group would march peacefully down one avenue, well-trained gangs would rampage down another, burning and looting. Former British Ambassador Anthony Parsons described one such incident, following the release of Ayatollah Taleghani:

> "Our conclusion was that the Taleghani demonstration had been arranged by religious leaders acting through local mosques, the crowd mainly comprising the artisan classes south of Tehran, the rank and file of the traditionalist movement. The burning had been organized, we felt, by the Mujahidin-e-Khalq (the People's Fighters), one of the extreme militant groups which had been conducting a war with SAVAK for years, perhaps in concert with the other main extremist groups, the Fedayin-e-Islam (those who Sacrifice Themselves for the Faith) with the possible assistance from the Communist (Tudeh) party. All three had the organization, the discipline, and the cohesion to carry out such an operation. In this context we stumbled on interesting evidence that, a few days before November 5th, the secondary schools, which had been rather aimlessly demonstrating ... had been infiltrated by adults who had directed and organized parties of children to burn and destroy when the time came."[38]

The situation in Iran became more volatile. I telephoned my brother and asked his permission to return. He refused and instructed me to remain in New York. Now I was convinced that someone, other than my brother, wanted to keep me away. Later, I learned that members of his government considered my return "highly undesirable." In certain circles—among those who believed my brother's departure was the best means of calming the growing agitation—it was feared that I (the "Black Panther") might be able to dissuade the Shah. I resigned myself to this involuntary exile—not the first in my lifetime. In 1951, Mossadegh had demanded that I be kept out of Tehran, for similar reasons, and he did succeed. However, this time I feared that much more catastrophic events were in the making, and that here, in New York, I could do nothing at all. In retrospect, I can see that this was a critical period, a time when the Carter people threw the full weight of the U.S. into the balance, pushing my brother into a position that can only be described as suicidal, at a time when the restoration of order was still possible.

Richard Sale has written: "If the Shah were to survive, October and November 1978 were the key months. It was now up to the Shah and his army. If the army was turned loose, especially after the creation of a military government in early November, sources claim that there would have been 10,000 casualties in Tehran alone, but the bulk of the public would have gone with the Shah ... Cottam agrees with this. They (the opposition) were not quite certain that we weren't going to back the Shah's army, he said."[39]

I know the truth is (and the British and American ambassadors recognize this in their books) my brother was opposed to the use of armed force. But our American ally, by its negotiation with and encouragement of the opposition groups, by its half-hearted (and privately disavowed) declarations of support for the Shah, by relentless pressure to loosen control in the face of growing anarchy, created a climate where the survival of my brother's regime was virtually impossible.

I was not to see him again until the autumn of 1979 when he came to New York for cancer treatment. Even in his weakened condition, with Khomeini calling for his life as ransom for the hostages, he could not stop thinking of the chaos and repression which had overtaken our country. I sat at his bedside, listening to him think aloud. "They (the Americans) don't understand," he said. "Even now, they don't understand. They believe that if I leave their country, they can make peace with this new regime ... they have no idea of what lies ahead."

As I tried to make sense of those final months, my brother said: "By October it was clear to me that the Americans wanted me out. The messages I received became more and more contradictory. The President would say one thing, and his ambassador would take another view. I felt they wanted me to leave, though what else they had in mind was a mystery. It is a bitter irony," he reflected, "that Iran was handed over to this Islamic Republic with an idea of containing Soviet expansion, that I was removed in the interests of human rights. Yet even now, with the seizure of the Embassy and the imprisonment of their citizens, the Americans can't see what they've done ... and persist in blaming me for their problems."

Now, years later, the factionalism and the failures of the Carter administration have been well-documented. As Michael Ledeen and William Lewis have written:

"Whatever the intentions of the President—and these remain unclear to the very end—both sides believed that the Carter administration would not tolerate any Iranian solution that was incompatible with the Human Rights policy as defined by the Human Rights Bureau in the State Department ... The Shah had been frustrated in his efforts to get a clear reading of American desires and intentions ... There was considerable conflict between the State Department and the National Security Council throughout the Iranian crisis, and the difference in the tone of the statements issuing from the White House and the State Department was early perceived by the Shah. By and large, the NSC—and Brzezinski in particular— believed that the nature of the Shah's regime was a distinctly secondary question, and that Iran was of such preeminent importance to American Middle-East policy that the Shah should be encouraged to do whatever was necessary to preserve control of the country. The State Department, on the other hand—especially Precht and the Secretary of State—was eager to establish that the old Kissingerian geopolitical view of the world had been abandoned in favor of a more moralistic approach. Thus

Vance gave Precht and the Human Rights Bureau Chief Derian full backing when they argued that the United States could not give support to repression in Iran. This view was also heartily endorsed by Ambassador Andrew Young and got the backing of Assistant Secretary of State for Near East and South Asian Affairs, Harold Saunders and Undersecretary of State for Political Affairs, David Newsom. Other potentially important actors carried little weight in the formation of Iran policy once the crisis got underway."[40]

In November 1978, I was still in New York at the UN. A friend called me from Washington and told me that the administration had just called in George Ball, the former Undersecretary of State, to make some recommendations. It was then that I felt exactly as my brother had a month before: that the Americans would soon abandon the Shah. Ball had, for a long time, been sympathetic to Iranian "liberals," former Mossadegh supporters, and active communists.

I was not the only one who saw special significance in the Ball report. Ibrahim Yazdi, the U.S. citizen who, for a time, was Khomeini's foreign minister, affirms that the report envisaged the establishment of an Islamic republic as a possibility—that this was the first time such a notation was introduced in high American circles. He says that until that point, the ambitions of the ayatollah's followers were limited to an "Islamic government" (which could have functioned under a regency council.[41]) Coincidentally, on November 7th, Khomeini announced from Paris that an Islamic republic would be formed, by force, if necessary.

The Egyptian journalist Mohamed Heikal describes, in his book, a meeting with Masud Rajavi, the head of the Mujahedeen, after the latter fled from Iran. Heykal says "he claimed it was George Ball's report on the Gulf which persuaded President Carter to abandon his support for the Shah."[42]

In an interview given in October, 1979, Ball himself admits that before responding to Carter's invitation, he had been convinced "for months that the Shah was finished and that the U.S.

should try to facilitate the transfer of power into some reasonably responsible hands."[43]

In Tehran, Ambassador Sullivan, in the course of his regular visits with my brother, reflected all the conflicts and contradictions within the Carter administration. Members of the embassy (who had long been in contact with both the lay and religious opposition) kept the opposition forces informed of these conflicts. The State Department attitude greatly encouraged the mullahs' intransigence, and in fact Mehdi Bazargan said: "Our revolution could never have succeeded without America!"[44] While the President and his NSC chief pushed my brother in one direction, the Secretary of State and other high-ranking officials pressed in another. Former Ambassador Sullivan, who describes these internal conflicts in his book, has accused Brzenzski of blocking the workings of the State Department and of preventing the Embassy from facing the situation—which was developing head on. Brzenzski, of course, has denied this (*Los Angeles Times*, Sept. 7, 1980)—and how Sullivan meant to "face the situation head on" remains a mystery. He never stopped telling my brother that he had the full backing of the U.S., and that he hoped he would re-establish order without slowing down his liberalization program. The internal rivalries within the administration resulted in a kind of paralysis, both in Washington and Tehran. American memoranda contradicted one another, from one day to the next—sometimes even within the same day.

President Carter, in his book, *Keeping Faith* (1982), complains that Sullivan's reports from Tehran were neither correct nor consistent. Sullivan wanted the U.S. to support Khomeini at the very moment that the Shah had called in Bakhtiar—at Washington's insistence. Carter goes on to say that a Sullivan memo informed him that Iranian military would not allow the Shah to leave the country, that they planned to have him live on an island in the Persian Gulf while they restored order (this has been confirmed by the Iranian military). Vance wanted to persuade the Army to let the Shah leave, while Brzezinski favored keeping the Shah in power. Sullivan believed that Khomeini takeover would lead to a democratic regime in Iran, and Carter complains that Sullivan only carried out his instructions half-heartedly, when he carried them out at all.

Simple confusion is not sufficient explanation of what happened in Iran. I believe that after 1977, the mullahs' revolution was in the hands of a group of Americans, who knew what they were doing (though they did not anticipate the results). Official documents seized by the "students" in November, 1979, record many contacts between American diplomats and members of the Iranian opposition (many articles published since 1979 agree, as do accounts I have gathered from Iranians in exile). In the second half of 1978, these contacts intensified, and from October on, members of the Embassy in Tehran, officials in the State Department, as well as the NSC, not to mention private "experts" consulted by Carter, were negotiating with members of the opposition, including those close to Khomeini. If Brzezinski continued to reassure my brother of America's support, it was not so much to reinforce the Shah's position, as to shore up America's image as a reliable ally. As for my brother, he had very little confidence at this point in any communications issued from America—and always asked Ambassador Sullivan for official confirmation of telephone conversations from the head of the NSC.

From Autumn 1978, there was, as Richard Sale writes: "... an unofficial network that was active in these talks between the administration and Khomeini, close enough to the government to be listened to, but far enough from Washington to be quickly and easily disowned."[45] Our ambassador in Washington had no information about this activity, but our friends in Paris recognized a number of American visitors to Neauphle-le-Chateau —including Ramsey Clark and Richard Cottam. As Richard Sale reports: "In the summer of 1978, Cottam accepted Yazdi's invitation to visit and interview Khomeini. It was Cottam who first discovered that the apex of the secret Khomeini apparatus in Tehran was Ayatollah Beheshti, from whose house came the flood of Khomeini tapes and speeches." Another member of the Washington-Iranian network was Iranian scholar, James Bill. As Sale reports: "In December 1977, he had already had contacts with the Ayatollah Taleghani and had at that time made a tour of south Tehran. Running into a colleague in Oman, Bill had said that the revolution was coming, that he was hopeful and that the U.S. had to be patient through the 'initial' discomforts that would accompany it." Sale documents further U.S. opposition connections: "Thomas Rick, a professor at Georgetown, was regularly seeing Ghotzbadeh in Europe. Henry Precht himself was in close touch with Mehdi Haeri, an Islamic scholar at Georgetown, whose father had been Khomeini's teacher at the theological school in Qum. Former U.S. ambassador to Iran, Armin Meyer had put Haeri in touch with Bill Miller of the Senate intelligence Committee through a State Department intermediary."

Documents seized in the American embassy show that by mid-1978, the U.S. officials in Iran were sending home alarming reports about the development of opposition activities. Yet in spite of these reports, Ambassador Sullivan pushed the Shah to free the dissidents and to continue the democratization—at the same time that U.S. officials on various levels were actively negotiating with the opposition. As John Stempel says: "Much of the blame can be laid on the Carter Administration, which not only misread the intelligence coming back from Iran, but actually encouraged the radical opposition against the Shah."[46] According to Ledeen and Lewis (*Washington Quarterly*, Spring 1980), Vance and the State Department, after November 1978, considered that the Shah "had outlived his usefulness" and that the crisis in Iran could only be resolved by his departure and the formation of a civil government based on wide support from the diverse opposition groups. Secretary of Energy Schlesinger believed that the U.S. should resort to the use of force, to demonstrate its support of the Shah—and to discourage intervention by other countries, particularly the Soviet Union and Libya. Brzezinski favored a show of strength, rather than actual military intervention. Carter did, in fact, consider this option, for in December, he did dispatch the aircraft carrier Constellation from its base in the Philippines, towards the Indian Ocean. But the President changed his mind and, without explanation, ordered the vessel, which was then halfway to its destination, to return to its home port.

These bits of information define rather well what was happening on the highest levels in Washington: A strong anti-Shah trend in the State Department; concern over the consequences of abandoning the Shah within the NSC; Carter's inability to formulate and direct a coherent policy. By December Carter was faltering even in giving lipservice support to my brother's government. During the course of a breakfast press meeting on the 7th, he was asked about the possibility of the Shah keeping his throne. Carter's answer: "I don't know. I hope so. This is something in the hands of the people of Iran"[47]

What I ask now is whether it is understood how much America's Iran policy (if it can be called that) was shaped by second-rank officials—and how the mullahs' "revolution" was implemented by a relatively small clique of Americans. To this end, there was, as Ledeen and Lewis point out, "a determined effort to portray Khomeini as a somewhat eccentric but basically admirable dissident or, in the words of Ambassador Young, 'a saint.' So strong was the desire to portray Khomeini as an acceptable, even democratic leader, that there was considerable disgruntlement in the State Department when three American newspapers published extensive accounts of Khomeini's writings. These articles containing excerpts from two of the ayatollah's books, revealed him to be a violently anti-Western, anti-American, anti-Zionist, and antisemitic individual, who was unlikely to offer the U.S. an attractive alternative to the Shah. Yet as late as the first week of February, 1979, when Khomeini was on the verge of returning to Tehran, Iran desk director Henry Precht told an audience of some 200 persons at a State Department 'open forum' that the newspaper accounts were severely misleading, and he even accused the *Washington Post* editorialist and columnist Stephen Rosenfeld of wittingly disseminating excerpts from Khomeini's book *Islamic Government*[48], that could be considered at best a collection of notes taken by students at worst a forgery. Precht did not read Farsi, but he had conversations with supporters of the ayatollah, who assured him that the accounts carried in the *New York Times* and the *Wall Street Journal*, as well as the *Washington Post* were inaccurate, and did not represent the views of Khomeini. Yet once

Khomeini seized power in Iran, both books were reissued in Farsi, and some passages were even more alarming than in Arabic. For example, in the 1973 Arabic edition of Islamic government, Khomeini had inveighed against 'Imperialists and Zionists'; in the 1979 Farsi edition, this had become a call for action against Christians and Jews. But Precht—and the State Department officials who relied upon him for information—did not consider the books authentic.

I must question whether it was only serious errors in judgment that led Precht and the anti-Shah group in the State Department to portray Khomeini as the solution to Iran's problems (not to mention as an advocate of human rights and a potential safeguard of America's regional interests). As Ledeen and Lewis revealed, the CIA had the ayatollah under surveillance from the time he first arrived at Neauphle-le-Chateau. Furthermore, American Embassy officials in Paris maintained regular contact with Bani-Sadr, Ghotzbadeh and Yazdi. Ledeen and Lewis add: "While there were graduations in the anti-Americanism of the various spokesmen, the Americans were under no illusion about the basic trust of the Khomeini group. Nevertheless there was conflicting 'information' from other sources (these other sources no doubt included Andrew Young, Ramsey Clark, as well as such independent experts as Richard Falk, Marvin Zonis, James Bill, etc.) suggesting that Khomeini was either a moderate or could be managed to permit policy makers to take a relatively optimistic view of the possibility that the ayatollah might return in triumph to Iran."[49]

Experts continued their apologies and their support for Khomeini after Washington had good reason to be uneasy about its choice. Richard Falk (who had earlier suggested that Khomeini's Iran might prove to be a "desperately needed model of humane governance") wrote: "One of Washington's problems in formulating a position toward Khomeini's movement may be its relative ignorance of the ayatollah's philosophy and of Shi'ite Muslim doctrine generally. It is entirely different from the harsher Sunni variety that currently prevails in Saudi Arabia, Libya, and Pakistan, among other Muslim nations. The entourage around Khomeini, in fact, has had considerable involvement in human rights activities and is committed to struggle against all forms of oppression. The constitution he proposes has been drafted by political moderates with a strong belief in minority rights. Contrary to the superficial reports in the American press about his attitudes towards Jews, women, and others, Khomeini's Islamic republic can be expected to have a doctrine of social justice at its core; from all indications, it will be flexible in interpreting the Koran, keeping that 'book of research' open to amendment and adaptation based on contemporary needs and aspirations."[50]

I was not at all surprised to read Ledeen and Lewis's view that Precht did more than actively promote Khomeini's candidacy for the leadership of Iran (both by presenting him in a false light and by encouraging the ayatollah's followers to take an uncompromising position), for he was also in a position to manipulate Carter's communications to the Shah during those last critical weeks. "Carter (during a late night telephone conversation from Camp David) had promised the Shah that he would issue a strong statement of support, but the actual document—prepared by Precht—was a mild one."[51] My brother considered this commitment from Carter of utmost importance. Frankly, at that point he did not have much choice but to carry on as if the alliance with the U.S. was fully functional. To break with the U.S. would have made Iran easy prey for the USSR. And, unlike me, my brother was always reluctant to consider the possibility of betrayal by those he considered friends. He did not understand what was happening within the American administration, as our ambassador in Washington did not go beyond cultivating the head of the NSC. So while there was mounting evidence to the contrary, he still believed in the value of a verbal commitment from an American president. The opposition shared this view, placing an even greater importance on Carter's words, weighing their own prospects on the basis of official and unofficial communications from Washington. It is clear now that if that statement of support promised by Carter had been forthcoming, if the wording had been strong and unequivocal, the political compromise that was then under discussion would have been accepted. But Precht had so vitiated the statement (Carter later termed this a "lack of enthusiasm") that the opposition immediately made inquiries as to the meaning. Yazdils son-in-law assured him that the President's statement of support could be disregarded, since it was "in form only." Opposition leaders in exile have confirmed that their reading of American policy was this: that the U.S. had decided to get rid of the Shah and to replace him with Khomeini. Any doubts they had disappeared after the Guadeloupe summit. In his memoirs, Ibrahim Yazdi reports that upon his return, Carter addressed a personal message to Khomeini, which was "the American government's first official contact with the Imam."[52]

FRENCH AND BRITISH SUPPORT OF KHOMEINI: Khomeini's choice of France as a place of residence after the Iraqi government prohibited his political activities was not pure chance. His advisors knew they could count on the support of a political base already established there by opposition groups. Shortly after his arrival in France, Khomeini began calling for revolution in Iran. Not a day went by without his exhorting the Iranian masses to demonstrate, the soldiers to desert, the workers to strike, etc. Some French Deputies and some newspapers called for the deportation of this "holy man" who was abusing his asylum and using France as a base of operations to launch a revolution in an allied country.

Yet the French government under Giscard D'Estaing closed its eyes to this abuse of the rights of asylum and allowed the ayatollah to continue his campaign against a government with which it maintained good relations. For a government to take such a position was unprecedented. Later, the French would claim that they asked Tehran if the Shah wished the ayatollah to be deported. I find this claim incredible. There were those in the French government who, like their counterparts in Washington, wanted the Shah out. They insisted that Khomeini's entourage was anticommunist and took the position that the west should hedge its backing of the Shah. This group reinforced the pro-Khomeini people in the Carter administration.

The situation in London was similar. I have already discussed the key role which the BBC played in disseminating

Khomeini's inflammatory speeches and coordinating his revolutionary activities. To this I will add only a statement by Sir
Anthony Parsons: "The British had a not undeserved reputation
for interfering in Iran's domestic affairs for over a century."[53]

THE LAST DAYS: WASHINGTON AND TEHRAN: In those final weeks before my brother's departure, the conflict between
Brzezinski and the State Department escalated. Brzezinski openly
attacked Precht, who was insisting on the Shah's ouster. He attempted to exclude Precht and other State Department
personnel from participation in important NSC discussions. The
Precht group countered by arranging a series of press "leaks,"
resulting in some articles which contained the contents of diplomatic cables, almost word for word. Some of the most
provocative items appeared in articles written by Bernard
Gwertzman in the *New York Times* (Ledeen and Lewis). In the
December 27th issue, for example, mention was made of the
administration's hope that the Shah would "continue to play an
important role" in leading Iran to a new government of "national
reconciliation." But at the same time, Gwertzman reported that
administration "officials" privately expressed the ultimate desir-
ability of the Shah's departure from the political scene.

Early in 1979, when my brother, at the insistence of the U.S.
named Shahpur Bakhtiar Prime Minister, the State Department
group which favored Khomeini leaked the content of secret talks
concerning Bakhtiar's appointment and expressed to the *Times*
its reservations about the new prime minister given "his limited
following in Iran." This was clearly an open invitation to the
mullahs to settle for nothing less than their "Islamic Republic."
Here, I find it interesting to note Cyrus Vance's account of this
period:

> "On January 2nd, the Shah told Ambassador Sullivan that
> he had decided to appoint Shahpour Bakhtiar, a promi-
> nent figure from the old National Front coalition, as
> prime minister. The Shah was highly skeptical of
> Bakhtiar's chances of winning support, but he wished to

give the civilian government alternative (pressed by the Americans) every possible chance.... The next day, January 3rd, Sullivan sent for my 'eyes only' a personal message in which he said that for the U.S. the 'moment of truth' had arrived in Iran. He reported that all the moderate elements in and out of the government agreed that the Shah must leave the country at once. He said, however, that a group of military officers were urging the Shah to forget Bakhtiar and apply the iron fist. Other Iranian generals were hinting at a coup to depose the Shah if he did not make some clear decision within the next few days. I agreed with Sullivan's conclusion that American interests, as well as those of Iran, required that the Shah leave immediately. The problem, as Sullivan observed, was that the Shah would depart only if he was advised to do so by the President. Sullivan emphasized that if the President intended to offer this advice, it must be done at once. If not, we could anticipate a military coup within a few days."[54]

With the passage of time, Vance's assessment bears some careful re-examination. His use of the word "moderate elements" assumes the same kind of political framework that the Carter administration constantly sought to re-create with its insistence on "liberal" values. His assumption that America's best interests would be served by the Shah's departure is questionable enough —but his assumption that he was also in a position to assess the best interests of Iran would be seriously disputed by countless Iranians. I must also question why the U.S. preferred a Khomeini government to military action. This has occurred several times in Turkey—without protest by Washington. (In fact, we can speculate that if the U.S. had followed a similar policy in Turkey, we might be seeing a Khomeini type government there today.) Officially, at the highest levels of the Carter administration, it had been decided that Bakhtiar—the prowestern "moderate"—should have the support of a united Iranian military force. To this end, it was decided to send General Robert

Huyser (then deputy to the Supreme Allied Commander in Europe) to Tehran.

THE HUYSER MISSION: Huyser arrived in Tehran on January 5, 1979, while President Carter met in Guadeloupe with French President Giscard D'Estaing, British Prime Minister Callaghan and West German Chancellor Schmidt. (It was during this meeting the French and Germans agreed with the American and British proposal for ousting the Shah.)

The Huyser mission was (and still is) shrouded in mystery, with many contradictory accounts given of its objectives and achievements.

I am at a loss to explain why my brother was not informed of Huyser's appointment or his arrival. Huyser saw the Shah once; accompanied by Ambassador Sullivan, he urged my brother to leave the country. My brother was informed by General Gharabaghi (then chief of staff) that Huyser had urged the Iranian military to meet with Bazargan, who would become Khomeini's first prime minister. According to Cyrus Vance, Huyser had been instructed to induce the military to support Bakhtiar's government. If the Bakhtiar government seemed unlikely to collapse, Huyser was to devise contingency plans to end the violence and disorder. Vance claims that Huyser found the military in a state of confusion, with some of its members suggesting an accommodation with Khomeini. Vance also says that Sullivan recommended that the U.S. bring about such an accommodation. On January 16th, Warren Zimmerman, chief of the American political section in Paris, met with Yazdi, while members of the military were in touch with Beheshti, Khomeini's representative in Tehran. On January 22nd, both Huyser and Sullivan were of the opinion that the U.S. should not support a military coup, that in the event Bakhtiar should fail, the Iranian army should be urged to negotiate with Khomeini. Vance adds that Brzezinski opposed any direct contract with Khomeini. Sepehr Zabih, an American professor of Iranian origin, contradicts this version. In his book, *Iran Since the Revolution*,[55] he states that the revolutionaries, led by Beheshti and Bazargan, were in daily contact with Huyser and urged him to ensure that the military would not instigate a coup. They argued that Bakhtiar's government was doomed, and that they, like the U.S. government, felt that post-revolutionary Iran would need a well-organized army to protect Iranian territorial integrity. They guaranteed the safety of U.S. military advisers and made assurances that sophisticated U.S.-made weaponry would not be compromised. John Stempel (then chief of the political section of the U.S. Embassy in Tehran) says that "Huyser had been sent to Iran by the President to assess the future of U.S. military programs in the country." For Ledeen and Lewis: "Huyser was sent to Tehran to ask the generals to transfer their loyalty to Bakhtiar, but without any guarantees for their future.... The Iranian generals were baffled by Huyser's mission. They, like the Shah, presumed that the U.S. had some sort of plan, but Huyser could not tell them what it was."

Ibrahim Yazdi gives yet another account in his book (*Last Moves in the Last Days*). The Iranian generals had decided to carry out a coup and to kill Khomeini, along with some of his aides. Yazdi says that Khomeini, from his residence in France, sent a message to Carter, warning that such a coup was not in the best interests of America, that it would be attributed to the U.S. and would be harmful to future relations between the two countries. Yazdi contends that Carter then sent Huyser to Tehran, to foil any possible coup and to prevent the murder of Khomeini. Perhaps the most throughly documented account of the Huyser mission was given by the Iranian general Amir Jussein Rabii, at his trial before the revolutionary military court, and reported in the Tehran daily, Ettelaat (March 28-30). Facing a certain death sentence, Rabii said that on January 10th, Huyser met with the highest ranking military men and told them bluntly that the Shah should go, that the Iranian people, like so many others, were no longer willing to accept an authoritarian regime. Huyser added that the U.S. and its European allies shared these feelings. After the Shah left the country, Huyser advised the generals to come to terms with Khomeini and provided them with a list of telephone numbers of Khomeini's representatives who were awaiting calls from the military and were ready to negotiate. He added that the military should encourage Bakhtiar to make contact with Khomeini's representatives.

Huyser's own testimony before a sub-committee of the U.S. Congress in June 1981 is somewhat baffling: He claims that the Iranian military was capable at the time of restoring order and security to the country and that he was puzzled as to why they did not attempt to do so.[56] The net result of the Huyser mission was, of course, the disintegration of the army and Khomeini's victory. As Sepehr Zabih says: "In retrospect, it is apparent that the victors in this drama were those shrewd negotiators for Khomeini. They succeeded in achieving the disintegration of the army, managed to insure against American intervention through the presence of General Huyser, and did so by reciprocating American acquiescence to the army's surrender by guaranteeing the safety of U.S. citizens."[57]

I cannot say with certainty that Huyser was sent to Tehran for the express purpose of neutralizing the army—and thus removing the only obstacle which stood in Khomeini's way, but this was in fact the net result of the Huyser mission. The Huyser mission, along with the press leaks, the official and unofficial messages emanating from Washington, told Khomeini very clearly, that there was no need for him to meet with or negotiate with Bakhtiar (he had previously agreed to such a meeting)—that in fact total victory was now assured. Almost immediately, there appeared in the streets of Tehran, the well-trained and well-armed "revolutionary" units, which had been prepared in secret and kept under cover, ready to spring into action after the army collapsed. Within a short time, Iran as we knew it would be destroyed. In its place, a monster would be born, would grow and strike out at those who helped deliver it.

6: DARK HORIZONS

THE KHOMEINI REVIVAL: Geneva, Switzerland. Our intelligence services reported a strange and unsettling incident. A commando group of Iranian students, led by specialists trained in Palestinian camps, storms the Iranian consulate and holds the staff hostage. The leader brandishes a pistol and forces a senior official to open the safe. Throwing aside the confidential correspondence and currency, he removes the stacks of blank passports and loads them into two sacks. He hands these over to another gunman, who leaves the consulate immediately and disappears into the passing crowd long before the police arrive. The "students" call a press conference. They announce that they have taken the consulate to focus public attention on the "Reign of Terror" in Iran and on the "bloody repression of the Shah's police." In fact, of course, it was the blank passports which were the real objective of the raid. Our government, trying to block the growing infiltration of foreign terrorist elements into the country, had decided to issue new passports, which were difficult to counterfeit. The "students," who belonged to a network created and directed by the Tudeh party, needed these passports to bring into Iran specialists in crowd control and manipulation, in terrorism and urban warfare.

Iran was, after a period of leftist guerrilla warfare, relatively quiet during the time which followed Carter's election. This was a conscious decision made by the Iranian left—to limit themselves (on the surface) to relatively peaceful activities in order to best take advantage of the new American administration's human rights policies. I believe this was the moment when the Tudeh Party began to implement its directive calling for the formation of a broad common front of all those who criticized the Shah's regime. This meant not antagonizing such groups as the National Front, the intellectuals, the Bazaar merchants, all of whom were against rioting and other forms of violence. 1977 was, therefore, relatively calm. As my brother's liberalization policies unfolded, the opposition groups slowly reemerged. The National Front regrouped itself around Sanjabi and the Liberation Movement around Bazargan. Together the two founded a Committee for the defense of Human Rights. They published manifestos, at first clandestinely, then openly; they demanded an end to all censorship, and they addressed letters to the Shah, demanding greater political liberties. When these activities were allowed to flourish, the opposition began to publish lists of "political" prisoners and demanded their release. Emboldened by this lenient atmosphere, the Tudeh Party, traditionally Iran's "outlaw" party, surfaced and began to show itself.

The various opposition groups were encouraged not only by my brother's liberalization, but also by the mounting campaign against him in the Western media. In 1977, more than 100 anti-Iranian publications circulated in the capitals of the West. In the United States, the *Iran Free Press* (which had been launched, according to our sources, with indirect funding from western intelligence services became particularly virulent in its attacks against my brother and the members of his family. (The editor of this paper had, in the late sixties, brought a business venture to one of my younger brothers. When this did not work out, he persisted in his attempts to extract money from him.)*

---

* The *Iran Free Press* ceased publication immediately following Khomeini's triumphant return to Tehran. In its last issue, it called for the nomination of Richard Cottam as U.S. Ambassador to Iran—no doubt as reward for services rendered.

According to our sources, several of these publications received subsidies from Libya. Still others received indirect aid, through multiple paid "subscriptions" from large oil companies and certain foundations.

My brother appointed a new prime minister in the summer of 1977. He did this in order to dramatize the change in his policies, to emphasize his determination to "clean house" and to decentralize the government. Inflation was running rampant through our economy, and the new prime minister, Jamshid Amouzegar, tried to bring it under control by taking Draconian measures. The first, the imposition of fixed prices, angered the Bazaari, who were already upset about the development of banking institutions that had taken over their traditional role as moneylenders. The second, the suppression of the subsidies ($80 million annually) which the State gave the clergy, provoked the anger of the mullahs. Beginning in the autumn of 1977, these two groups joined the secular opposition. The Ayatollah Shariat-Madari, a religious conservative, began speaking out against my brother's modernization policies. Other mullahs followed suit, preaching this criticism in their mosques. This development did not suit the leaders of the Tudeh Party, who had found refuge in East Germany, or the clerics of Khomeini's entourage, who had found refuge in Iraq. Their objectives could be effectively blocked by a successful coalition of the National Front and the movement inspired by Shariat-Madari which favored a constitutional compromise. They were even more concerned when they saw that several members of the Carter administration favored this coalition, which was seen as "moderate." Yet in the autumn of 1977, Khomeini's followers and the Tudeh leftists represented a tiny minority in the country, not capable of organizing or controlling a serious opposition movement. For this, they needed specialists trained in the logistics of urban warfare: Professionals trained in Palestinian, Cuban and Libyan camps. The passports stolen from our consulate in Geneva served this purpose. To minimize the possibility of detection by our police, these agents used the special charters run by Iran Air throughout the summer to transport groups of students who came home to spend their holidays with their families.

By autumn of 1977, a large number of terrorists and specialists trained in crowd manipulation found their way into Iran. Some belonged to Tudeh-related groups, others to Khomeini's Islamic networks. The alliance between the these two groups began to solidify, in Europe and in the Middle East. Sadegh Ghotzbadeh was one of its main architects. Through Musa Sadr, the Imam of the Shi'ites of Lebanon, he kept close contact with Khomeini. Through Arafat and the PLO, he developed ties with the Tudeh and European communists. In the United States, however, where Ibrahim Yazdi was busy convincing American officials of his ability to speak for the Iranian opposition, this alliance did not quite take hold. There, the Muslim student associations remained separate. Yazdils organization acted independently, while the associations receiving Libyan subsidies cooperated with the Iranian students of the communist "Confederation." Our students abroad have always been receptive to agitators of the left and right, as well as to agents of various secret services. I have already told about the Student Associations in America, the Committee for Artistic and Intellectual Freedom (created by Reza Baraheni), and the Frankfurt to based Iranian students. To this list I can add the Islamic Student Associations; the Islamic Marxists; the "Terhrani Group" (after the name of its Marxist leader, Mehdi Khanbaba Tehrani); the Democratic Organization of Iranian Youth, a Tudeh Party offspring in Western Germany. Other powerful outside forces during this period were organizations linked to the Washington based Institute for Policy Studies, the radical think tank which had supported Cuba and Vietnam, and which had built an influential network of friends in Congress, in the media and in the Carter administration.

Reliable sources have told me that most of IPS's considerable budget was provided by the Rubin Foundation (set up by Samuel Rubin, the Marxist heir to the Faberge fortune), which also contributed to other radical groups. One such organization was the Transnational Institute (TNI)—which, I have learned, was a principal coordinator in the campaign against my brother.[58] In early 1978, according to the same source, several TNI researchers became active in the campaign against my brother's government. The most prominent of these people: Fred Halliday (who had written an apologia of the Marxist regime of south Yemen titled "Arabia Without Sultans"); Michael Klare (a leftist specialist on militarism and disarmament, who contributed information on our arms deals with the U.S.); Joe Sort, a staunch supporter of the most militant Palestinian groups (he was a key speaker at the "International Symposium on Zionism as a Racist Phenomenon" held in Baghdad, in November 4, 1976). With the help of various leftist groups, an "International Symposium on Iran" was held on May 6-7, 1978 in Brussels. Participants included representatives of European communist parties, Iranian opposition groups and the British Labour Party. Fred Halliday addressed the conference. Among the resolutions adopted: One calling for more publicity on alleged human rights violations in Iran. At the same time, the American Friends Service Committee (AFSC) organized hearings against the shipment of American arms to Iran with Michael Klare as speaker. In September 1978, the Soviet controlled World Federation of Trade Unions (WFTU), based in Prague, issued a statement calling on all workers to intensify solidarity actions in support of the Iranian workers' struggle for a decent life and human rights. This followed the Tudeh-directed strike by Iranian oil workers, who were at the time among the best paid in the world. The Soviet-subsidized Iranian magazine NAVID had published, a few months before, the article entitled "The Tudeh Party and the Muslim Movement," which urged a broad based opposition front, with the mullahs as the vanguard. And so, the alliance between Red and Black was building—within the country and without.

THE SHAH'S ILLNESS: The cessation of terrorist activities in 1977 had caused some uneasiness, some apprehension that the period of quiet was but a prelude to something more serious.

Yet my brother continued to press on with his liberalization policies. This baffled me, as I know it did those of his advisers who were loyal to the monarchy. Knowing the psychology of our people, I felt instinctively that this was the wrong time for such widespread relaxation of power. In a country like ours, people identify government with personalities rather than abstract ideals or theories. Traditionally the government is seen as a father figure rather than as a faceless bureaucracy. A relaxation of authority in a time of unrest like this could only be interpreted in one way: that the "father" was seriously ailing and therefore not long for this world. Yet no matter how often I raised this issue, my brother would not change his course. In retrospect, a number of observers have concluded that this was one of several critical—and wrongly made—decisions. Anthony Parsons, the last British ambassador to our court, believed that it was my brother's determination to institute political democracy which caused his fall and facilitated Khomeini's accession to power.[59]

I know that in the end it was the acceleration of this policy at a time of violent upheaval, the increasing pressure to do more of the same by our allies (who had already begun to make accommodations with Khomeini), which ruptured the centralized government structure created by my father then built upon by my brother. Since my brother would not—or could not, in the eyes of his people—exercise governmental authority, the path was cleared for a new father figure, one who laid claim to divine authority.

So many times, as a frustrated bystander, I asked why this was allowed to happen. And when finally I discovered my brother's illness, I understood the thinking behind the choices he made. Knowing he was seriously ill, my brother had hoped to push forward a true constitutional monarchy, which he could then pass on to his son. He kept the news of his illness to himself, fearing that it might precipitate disorder and disintegration in Iran. Later, near the end of his life, he told me that he regretted this decision, that he should have at least informed a few of his closest advisers.

I feel so much sorrow and pain when I think of what this choice cost him. I realized that in a very real sense, he sacrificed his life to keep the secret. He chose the most conservative forms of treatment, those that would control the symptoms of his cancer, rather than the more radical therapies that might have cured the disease in its early stages. And while he alone understood why it was important to complete the task he had given himself, his government did not. Members of our law enforcement agencies felt demoralized and handicapped by his orders. How could they keep order if they were compelled to ignore open provocations? Unanswered questions filtered down to the inhabitants of the capital and made them uneasy. Why was the government answering challenges to its authority with more freedom? Even the opposition was puzzled for a time. I have been told that many of our countrymen thought at first that this was a clever tactical maneuver, that the police were biding their time, allowing the opposition to show itself so that they might more effectively crush it. In pro-government circles, there was a general uneasiness. The wealthy began to transfer their fortunes abroad. Among officials and civil servants, the most pressing questions were: What is going on and why? Wild rumors of all kinds began circulating through Tehran. When I brought these to my brother, he was evasive and told me my imagination was running away with me. Today I deeply regret not having pressed the matter so that I might have shared the burden he was carrying alone. But old habits are difficult to break. Since childhood, I had always gone to him in times of trouble and taken comfort from his calm and determination. Over the years we had weathered so many crises. I'm certain I wanted to believe that we would do so again.

KHOMEINI REAPPEARS: In September 1977, shortly before I made my annual trip to the UN, I spoke with a friend who worked with Iran-Air, organizing student charters. "This has been a strange year," he said. "Our planes are full of empty seats."

"People travel less in autumn," I suggested.

"I don't mean our regular flights," he said. "I'm talking about our student flights. It's as if a lot of them are staying in Iran. We already have a state of discontent at our universities. If these students from foreign universities were to join the local students, we could see the kind of troubles they've had in Europe." That possibility troubled me, but what actually happened that year was far more serious. Using the passports stolen from our Consulate, scores of well-trained Tudeh and Khomeini agents of various nationalities (mainly Palestinian) entered Iran, made contact with local groups and prepared for the months ahead. This was the period when the alliance between "Red" and "Black" which my brother had talked about was actually meshing within our country.

During my years in exile, I have had many conversations with other exiles, intellectuals and professionals who had once attacked the monarchy. Embittered now, they denounced the mullahs for stealing "their" revolution. I have little patience with this claim, for it was the mullahs who actually launched the revolt. The intellectuals' mistake was to align themselves with the clerics, despite the disastrous precedents of the 19th century. The first riot, which broke out in Qum on January 7, 1978, and which served as a springboard for other incidents, involved clerics alone. It came one day after one of Tehran's large daily newspapers published an anti-Khomeini article.

So it was at the beginning of 1978 that Khomeini, who had long ago faded from the Iranian political scene and who was no longer seen as a serious threat by our government, was revived as a major force. From his exile in Najaf, he launched his cassette campaign, and suddenly his speeches were everywhere. A vast army of mullahs, preaching in some 60,000 mosques, worked to mobilize the masses against modernization. In this way, the Shah, symbol of modernization was pitted against God, and the mullahs commanded the faithful to side with God. At the time, a number of observers mentioned the "non-violent" character of the clerical campaign. In fact, the crowd specialists who had infiltrated the country did manage to transform the rioting mobs of early January into orderly and disciplined demonstrators. But beyond the marchers who chanted slogans in peaceful fashion, the terror which would soon rule Iran had begun. Hundreds of banks and liquor stores (the use of interest and alcohol being forbidden by Islam) were destroyed by Khomeini's supporters. Public and government property was looted. Casinos and nightclubs were razed. Cinemas, being places that propagated Western values, became popular targets for arsonists.

By the summer of 1978, tens of thousands of Iranian students returned, swelling the ranks of demonstrators. Under the pressure from the White House, and despite the pleadings of his generals, my brother surrendered his authority by degrees. According to Carter, the only acceptable solution to Iran's problems lay in appeasing those who controlled the mobs. In yielding to Washington's pressure, my brother did not realize that his principal ally had already decided on his successor.

Her Imperial Highness Princess Ashraf Pahlavi.

My son, Prince Shahriar, Shah Reza Pahlavi heir to the throne of Iran.
Photo courtesy Captain Said Zangench of thc Imperial Iranian Navy.

Princess Ashraf Pahlavi with Senator Daniel Patrick Moynihan at the United Nations.

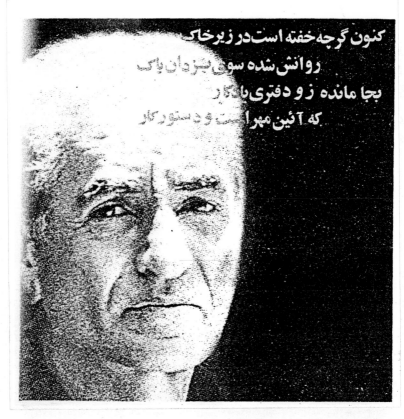

کنون گرچه خفته است در زیر خاک
روانش شده سوی یزدان پاک
بجا مانده زو دفتری یادگار
که آئین مهر است و دستور کار

H.I.M Mohammed Reza Pahlavi during his last days in Egypt.

Beneath the ground his
        body lays
But with God almighty
        his soul stays
He left us his profound legacy
Which is a motto of kindness
        and a road to follow

Photo courtesy of The IRANIAN Newspaper, Vancouver, B.C.

7: THE ENTHRONEMENT OF KHOMEINI

KHOMEINI RETURNS: For me the years of exile have been years of loss—of family, of progress and work, of friends and of country. All in the name of religion. My first vivid glimpse of what lay in store for us came during my last trip home in the fall of 1978. I had been in Russia, attending a conference of the World Health Organization in Alma Ata in Kazakhestan. When I left Alma Ata and flew to Tehran's Mehrabad Airport, I was confronted by mobs of demonstrators around the Shahyad Monument. The roads to my house in Saadabad were blocked, I had to make the trip by helicopter. As I flew over the Shahyad Monument, I saw that one corner was completely black. And then a moment later I realized that this black mass was a crowd of Iranian women, draped in the mournful chador worn by their grandmothers. It was a terrible sight, for Iran's women had reached, by Middle Eastern standards, very high levels of emancipation. This black garment seemed to me not the return to modesty preached by the fundamentalists, but rather the voluntary surrender of all the rights we had worked so long and so hard to achieve.

I can see why these women acted as they did and how badly they were used by the mullahs. This clerical revolution is about the achievement of political power, yet it uses the highly emotional content of religion to gain the acceptance of people who, in the clear light of reason, would not choose this as a way of life. The covering of our women was a highly visible and very successful propaganda tool for the mullahs. Those who could not be persuaded to cover themselves for God's sake were forced to do so by physical violence. Many of our women, who voluntarily supported the mullahs, have now realized that they have traveled back in time to a period when a woman was said to have "more hair than brains," to a time when women were regarded as both the property and perpetual wards of men. Six years ago, this was not made clear to them. They were enlisted by the mullahs as comrades in arms, as fellow revolutionaries in a holy cause—like so many groups who have since either been eliminated or mercilessly repressed by that cause. Not all of Khomeini's allies were enlisted on the basis of religious solidarity. The powerful and necessary link he made with the PLO was forged on the basis of very practical considerations. Since Khomeini's goal was total and absolute rulership, he needed an army of trained enforcers, and Arafat, whose personal political fortunes had waned after the Camp David accord and the setback in Lebanon, was ready to be a source of supply. In return, he gained a power base in Iran, two dollars in royalties on every barrel of oil exported by Iran and Khomeini's cooperation in the "war" against Israel. This alliance surfaced only after Khomeini made his triumphal return to Tehran, which I followed carefully from exile. It was no great surprise to me when Arafat arrived on February 16, 1979. With an escort of Iranian Air Force, of the kind given to honor foreign heads of state on official visits, he landed in Tehran. As he embraced the old ayatollah, he joked that this was the first time American war planes were not trying to shoot at him. A moment later, he announced to reporters: "At this all-important moment, I vow in the name of the fighters and revolutionaries, to liberate, altogether the Palestinian territory under the leadership of the great Imam Khomeini." Khomeini's guest and ally was lodged in a luxurious villa he called "the house of Jews," because it had housed the Israeli mission during my brother's reign. The PLO ambassador was also authorized to open offices in all Iranian cities. Designated "security advisers," the Palestinians, under the command of Abu Jihad, were stationed in ministries, universities, and public places. A special branch provided what was termed, under a secret agreement, "operational services"—the disposal of troublesome opposition, in and outside of Iran.[60] In one of many gestures of solidarity, Khomeini and Arafat publicly declared their common goals. From Khomeini: "Now that the monarchy has been overturned, my next target is Israel." And from Arafat: "We feel much stronger since the success of the Iranian revolution ... The road to Palestine passes through Tehran ... The popular movement in Iran will overturn the balance of power in the Middle East."[61]

I learned a year later (from a U.S. Joint Chief of Staff report) that more than 15,000 PLO officers and trained specialists were serving in Iran's armed forces. From a Joint Chief of Staff source, I learned that the mullah's government was paying nearly $400 million for PLO services. I found the reaction of the U.S. intelligence community curiously limited. Of course there was immediate concern about the advanced American and British equipment sold to us in recent years. They concluded, correctly I'm sure, that whatever secret equipment left intact at our monitoring stations had since fallen into Soviet hands, along with the instruction manuals.[62] But equally dangerous, as far as regional stability is concerned, is the Palestinian presence in Iran. Since 1979, many of Khomeini's allies have fallen by the wayside. The Palestinian remain well-entrenched, although I know that some of Khomeini's own advisers have become uneasy about their presence.

WHO IS KHOMEINI AND WHAT IS THE ISLAMIC REPUBLIC?: Since December 1978, when Khomeini reappeared, as the uncontested leader of the opposition, there was widespread questioning and confusion about the personality and intentions of the "holy man from Qum." The confusion was no less among members of the Carter administration, which had found him an ideal candidate for leadership. Among the secret documents seized by the students who took the American Embassy, there is one communication which describes Khomeini as a religious fanatic ... a most unlikely choice for the task which lay ahead. There is, however, yet another document which gives a better clue to what America's hopes were. It expressed confidence that the clergy, politically unsophisticated as they were, inexperienced in the exigencies of modern technology, would, once in power, be receptive to advice and assistance (such advice and assistance would, of course, be American). The assumption was that the clergy would see the value of America's friendship and business would go on as usual. This illusion was fed at first by a fairly benign posture on Khomeini's part, and by the reassurances of his secular partners, who saw the importance of telling the world that the new government would be a model of reason and of human rights.

I could not help but smile at the grim ironies of Ibrahim Yazdi's comments in *Penthouse*. At the very moment when Khomeini's men were destroying all newspapers which voiced the slightest criticism of the Islamic Republic, Yazdi said: "Liberty under the Islamic Republic is deeper than what you have in Western societies ... (our) newspapers are not all for the Islamic Republic, for Khomeini.... We know that some of these papers are still working for the old regime under new covers. They are highly critical of the situation, and the government has done nothing to stop them or tell them what to do. They are free to say anything they want.... Women may wear the chador or not wear it. This is their choice. The rights of Iranian women will be guaranteed by the constitution. There can be no compromise on this."[63] To the same magazine (a strange choice for a holy man), Khomeini said: "Islam is freedom. Freedom from injustice, freedom from exploitation, freedom for brotherhood."[64]

Earlier in the year Sadegh Ghotzbadeh (the man who would suggest to the Americans that they assassinate my brother as a solution to the hostage crisis—and who would himself later be shot by his mentor) introduced this theme of Islam and freedom: "Religion has never been put aside in the lives of Muslims without suffering and misery replacing it.... The new Iranian regime, founded on Islamic instruction and on the experiences of the Prophet and Ali, will offer complete freedom to all, in order to achieve the enlightenment (fulfillment) of all.... In the course of history, the oppressed peoples have always called on the liberals. That's what Hussein did, in the history of Islam, the day of the Ashura (the massacre of the Imam and his family). This appeal is not limited to any one moment in history. It is destined to all humanity at all times. Today in this critical moment in its history, the Iranian people once again issues this appeal to all the liberals of the world."[65] The French philosopher, Michael Foucault (who changed his opinion before his death), believed there was no confusion whatever as to the nature of the Islamic Republic: "I often hear that the definitions of the Islamic government are imprecise. To me they appear, on the contrary, to be of a very familiar clarity.... They are the basic propositions of bourgeois or revolutionary democracy ... when the Iranians speak of Islamic or revolutionary democracy.... When the Iranians speak of Islamic government ... it is first of all a question of a movement which tends to give the traditional structures of Islamic society a permanent role in political life ... (The Islamic government) ... is that which would allow for the introduction of a spiritual dimension into political life... (such a government) would provide that political life would not be an obstacle to spirituality (religion) but its receptacle (guardian)."[66] In the United States, Richard Falk dismissed any suggestion that Khomeini might be a fanatic: "This seems certainly and happily false ... (The ayatollah) may yet provide us with a desperately needed model of humane governance for a third-world country."[67] An equally glowing report came from Canadian author

Rubin Carlesen, who wrote after a visit with Khomeini: "He was a flowing mass of light that penetrated into the consciousness of each person in the hall ... He was that singular reality which could expand my consciousness, purify my brain, and leave in his wake the sense of an undiminishable grace ..."[68]

My files are filled with hundreds of similar evaluations and speculations about the enlightenment and purity of Khomeini and his government. There were fewer who raised questions as to the nature of his new regime. In France, Maxime Rodinson wrote: "There is neither improbability nor shame in revolutionary movements in the name of religion... But we must be vigilant before their victories and keep a critical stance towards the propaganda of intellectuals from within and the credulity of those on the outside ... Religions are not dangerous because they preach belief in God, but because they have no remedies for the inherent evils of society except moral exhortations ... In power, they (religions) succumb to the temptation to impose, in the name of moral reform, an order of the same name."[69] Even before Khomeini returned to Iran, Professor Vatikiotis, Middle East specialist at the University of London said: "Anyone who suggests setting up an Islamic state or an Islamic republic faces great difficulties. Some of the difficulties are theoretical, but nonetheless important. According to Islam, God is sovereign. No people or their representatives can have sovereignty under an Islamic state. To talk about an Islamic republic is a contradiction in terms. The key premise in a republic is the sovereignty of the people or their representatives. That's not done in strict Islamic terms. Also in Islam, no man can legislate, because legislation was done once and for all through the prophet Muhammed in the Koran. However, it's not so simple in a world of longstanding nation-states. An Islamic state would have to deal with rivalries between the superpowers and fit into a world economic order."[70] In all the years Khomeini has been writing and preaching, he has been perfectly consistent, albeit often in a hysterical and ranting fashion, on three issues: His hatred for the Pahlavis, for Israel—and for the United States. In 1963, he denounced my brother for his ties to the U.S., charging that Iran had "sold itself" and that these ties had "reduced Iran to the level of a colony." In 1967, he said, "Let the American President know that in the eyes of the Iranian nation he is the most repulsive member of the human race today because of the injustice he had imposed on our Muslim nation." During the same year he also declared that he had been exiled because of his anti-American position. This was simply not true—but it was reason enough for Khomeini to include America in his personal revenge. Yet in early 1979, American officialdom preferred to view Khomeini as a reasonable and humane "moderate." From *Newsweek* (January 29, 1979): "Some U.S. officials detect a more moderate tone in Khomeini's recent statements. And they express the hope that if he becomes a political leader, Khomeini may prove to be somewhat more pragmatic than his militant utterances as a Muslim holy man might indicate."

POLITICAL SMOKESCREENS: In the early days of his regime, Khomeini was careful to present a facade of moderation and conciliation (the Shi'ite concept of Takye allows the believer to hide his true thoughts and intentions). Though his victory appeared to be overwhelming, it did not assure his reign. Once my brother had left, the alliance of diverse opposition forces could not survive for long. The ethnic minorities—Kurds, Baluchis, Arabs, Turkomans, etc.—were demanding autonomy, all the more so since most of them were Sunnis. The communists, though they lent their allegiance to the ayatollah and temporarily took the green flag of Islam, were fundamentally committed to the hammer and sickle. The Mujahiddin and their guerilla forces were a separate faction. Then there were the Muslim masses, who were basically divided into three factions: the leftists, under Ayatollah Teleghani; the centrists (moderates) under Ayatollah Shariat Madari (this group included the middle classes and the bazaar merchants); and the rightists, a group made up of property owners, chiefs of large tribes and a number of ayatollahs. The Shi'ite clergy were not a united power block; most of the more powerful ayatollahs contested the supreme authority of their colleague, Khomeini. Still another faction was the Imperial Army, which was still intact, despite the defection of some units. For Khomeini, those early days were not the time to openly antagonize any group—or any foreign powers, particularly not the U.S. and the USSR. To achieve his goal of a theological dictatorship (and this intention, too, is laid out in his writings), a temporary smokescreen was necessary. On the advice of Ayatollah Beheshti, a shrewd political strategist, he appointed Mehdi Bazargan prime minister on February 5, 1979, while Bakhtiar still occupied the office of President of the Council of Ministers. The 70 year old Bazargan was ideally suited to the role of front man. He had spent a little time in prisons, and, in 1977, he had begun working with opposition groups. His training as an engineer gained the support of the technocrats, his prosperous business ventures, the support of businessmen and merchants. His pious past and his authorship of Islamic pamphlets made him acceptable to the clergy and the Muslim masses. He had visited Khomeini at Neauphle-le-Chateau and recognized his leadership. His previous contacts with the Americans (who had encouraged him to form his Committee for the Defense of Human Rights in 1977), his European dress and manner, were reassuring to the West. In short, his natural moderation, his past opposition to my brother, his religious devotion would satisfy everyone as to the "moderate" nature of the new government and give the ayatollah time to create the revolutionary institutions which would shift all effective power to him.

And as for the last days of the Bakhtiar government—under the best of circumstances, this last appointee of my brother's would have had a difficult time holding on. But instead of attempting some practical measures to consolidate the position of the civilian government, he spent an inordinate amount of time on self-congratulation. To the French journalist Georges Menant, he said: "Look what I have already accomplished. In a few short weeks, I have gotten rid of the Shah. I have reestablished freedom, abolished censorship, suppressed the SAVAK.

That's democracy ... People are going to realize that sooner or later ... The intellectuals, the bourgeoisie, the military leaders, everyone who makes the country run is beginning to understand that the Islamic Republic would be a 'leap in the dark.' If the strikes do not stop, the ayatollah will soon appear as the destruction of the nation. And besides, even among the mullahs, people are starting to oppose him. His authoritarianism, his ego, his manner of presenting himself like the moon surrounded by the stars, all that creates more and more jealousy."[71] To a reporter from *Le Matin* who asked Bakhtiar how he would react to Khomeini's appointment of Bazargan, he declared he would respond with a single word: "Shit!" This is exactly the kind of response Khomeini wanted. While Bakhtiar deluded himself with his "successes" and allowed himself to be photographed in his office and swimming pool, Khomeini was cutting the ground out from under him and building up his own man, Bazargan. And while he left the two seculars to confront one another, the ayatollah and his clerical supporters began creating their own government—the (secret) Council of the Revolution; the neighborhood Komitehs by which local populations could be controlled—and instituting techniques of intimidation: Arbitrary searches of homes, arrests without warrants, occupation of buildings, confiscation of goods, torture and summary of executions without trial. At the same time, the Palestinians and Iranians trained in their camps were forming the units of the Pasdarans, the Revolutionary Guards, which supplanted the regular police force and, in many cases, the regular army. Soon Bazargan understood the role he had been assigned. To whomever would listen, he repeated: "They've put a knife in my hand, but it's a knife with only a handle. Others are holding the blade."

There was a long interview with Oriana Fallaci in which Khomeini said: "Who's in command today in Iran? If I were to say I'm in command, that wouldn't be true ... Khomeini is in command, with his revolutionary Komitehs, his revolutionary councils, his revolutionary guards, and his relationship with the masses ... And then there are the revolutionary tribunals, the religious authorities who, with the pretext of carrying on the revolution, are administering many cities and causing all kinds of problems ..."[72] Frustrated though he was, Bazargan knew he could not resign without endangering his life and those of his followers. On this matter, our Iranian tradition is clear: No one leaves the office without being discharged. The system does not allow escape routes.

This was a particularly difficult time for me, for I had only recently learned of the seriousness of my brother's illness. But some days, it was hard to focus on personal problems, as I read and heard stories of what my country was being subjected to. Confident with his early successes, in the country and in the press, Khomeini unleashed a horde of mullahs and armed thugs on Iran. To the extent that he felt the need to defend himself, he brandished lists of crimes committed by the Shah and the U.S. which were never before seen in Iran, while he ranted about my brother's so-called excesses. Though he had condemned the SAVAK, he quickly launched his own secret police, the SAVAMA, made up of former SAVAK agents and led by Palestinian terrorists.

My younger son Shahriar was one of his early victims, shot in the back by Palestinian gunmen on a Paris street. The horror of that day—the phone call from my daughter Azadeh—the news I could not really take in for months—it has never really left me. I felt a bitter rage when I read the words of Khomeini's chief executioner, the mullah Khalkhali, as he boasted of the crime to *Le Point*. "To tell the truth," the madman said, "it was his mother we were after... But he was the one were able to get to."

Over the years I have mourned so many losses. So many friends, patriots who served their country well, murdered. I mourn, too, for Iran, and I sometimes feel this is all a terrible dream, this regime which has, as one of its central themes, the annihilation of 25 centuries of civilization. I wonder how it was possible for anyone to doubt Khomeini's intentions after he began speaking more freely to the press, justifying every new horror as necessary to his goal. To Oriana Fallaci, he said: "We are an infant of six months. Our revolution is only six months old. And it came to a country devoured by suffering like a field of wheat infested by locusts. We are only at the beginning of our route. And what do you expect from an infant of six months who is born in a field of wheat infested by locusts, after two thousand five hundred years of poisoned harvests? We cannot wipe out this past in a few days, a few months, or even a few years. We need time."[73] The "poisoned harvests" the ayatollah referred to are the sum total of my country's history, from the days of Cyrus the Great. Symbolizing his intentions, he set his mullahs to destroy the ruins of Persepolis. He also attempted, at the beginning of his reign, to abolish our ancestral new year and to replace it with the date of the Hegira, but popular uproar obliged him to put this project aside.

KHOMEINI'S JUSTICE: One of the most chilling aspects of Khomeini's reign has been the introduction of his personal interpretations of Islamic justice. Now that his revolutionary "infant" has passed its sixth birthday, his Islamic tribunals are no different from his Revolutionary Tribunals of the first hours. There are no lawyers, no appeals. It is a revival of eighth century justice, but without the tempering force of mercy. All the judicial processes of the past 12 centuries have been rejected. To be a judge in Khomeini's Iran, the only requirement is to be a mullah. The reform instituted by my father in 1925, whereby the administration of justice was taken from the mullahs and assigned to tribunals independent of the executive and the legislature, was abolished, along with modern codes of civil, criminal and commercial law, which had governed our society for more than half a century. In place of the penal code and the code of criminal procedure, which guarantees to the accused rights, similar to those which exist in all the civilized countries of the world, Khomeini instituted the LAW OF THE TALON.[74] When Khomeini was questioned more recently on the subject of his hasty trials, he answered: "Evidently you westerners don't know, or pretend you don't know who those executed were ...

What were we supposed to do? Pardon them? Let them leave? We gave them the right to defend themselves, to answer to the accusations. They could answer whatever they wanted. But once their guilt was proven, what need was there for an appeal?"[75] In a speech four months earlier, after hearing about protests by various human rights groups, the old man said scornfully: "Those people should have been killed the first day. No one would have said anything. There is no possible objection to the trials of these people. They are criminals. Criminals should not be tried. They should be slaughtered. Still earlier, in 1981, the new attorney-general of the revolution, the Hojatoleslam Tabrizi, had advocated an even more expeditious procedure, for dealing with those who 'participate in demonstrations against the government,' inviting the authorities to execute each night the demonstrators arrested during the day and to finish off the wounded.[76] The number of summary executions since the mullahs took power has been estimated at more than 40,000, the number of political prisoners at more than 150,000."[77]

In a speech he made in Tehran on May 20, 1980, the same Khomeini said: "All drug dealers should be executed. No mercy, no extenuating circumstances are called for in their cases." Apparently the "no mercy" condition is a universal one. After the flight of fallen president Bani-Sadr and Massoud Rajavi, leader of the Mujahiddin, Khomeini's men launched a savage campaign against their followers, described here by the London *Sunday Times*:

> "Security forces have orders to shoot armed opponents on the spot, dispensing with formalities of arrest and trial. A nightly TV spot is devoted to people denouncing their executed sons or daughters and saying they would refuse to pick up their 'satanic' corpses. Islamic associations are taking whole page ads in newspapers to express their gratitude to the Ayatollah Khomeini for 'weeding out the enemies of Allah.'"[79]

Elsewhere in the same newspaper:

"It is difficult to distinguish between executions for political reasons and those resulting from 'religious crimes,'
since all the victims are described as the 'enemies of
Allah'… The majority of those executed (recently) were
aged between 18 and 35. The youngest victim was Sahra
Mossayebi, a nine year old girl executed in Tehran last
June on charges of attacking the revolutionary guards.
The legal execution age is nine for girls and fifteen for
boys. The oldest person executed was the Kurdish poet
and politician Allameh Vahidi, who was 102 … Ethnic
minorities were among the first to suffer executions in
the Islamic Republic. The Kurds claim to have lost at least
1,000 and more Turkomans are known to have been
executed. Among religious minorities, the Bahai sect has
lost 160 people, either executed or murdered by revolutionary Komitehs. The Shaikhis have recorded 49
executions, the Jews have lost 27 and the Christians 14,
while the tiny Sabean minority have lost eight."[80]

Journalist Oriana Fallaci questioned Khomeini in September of 1977 about a story she had read in local Tehran
newspapers that a pregnant 18 year old girl had been executed
in Behshar on charges of adultery. "Pregnant?" the old man
shouted. "That's a lie—just like the story of the severed breasts
(referring to a story that was circulating at the time—that female
'enemies of Allah' were tortured by cutting off their breasts). In
Islam, pregnant women are not executed." When Fallaci pressed
the matter, saying that there had been a debate regarding the
case on the official television station, Khomeini responded: "If
that's true, that means she deserved what she got. The woman
must have done something else, something serious … Anyway,
that's enough talk of all this. You are tiring me. These are not
important matters."

KHOMEINI'S REVOLUTION: PHASE TWO: While Bazargan foundered for nine months, the Ayatollah Beheshti was assembling his Islamic Republican Party, which would take over all decision-making power and become the instrument for carrying out Khomeini's wishes. However, as a former collaborator with the Shah's regime who at one point had been subsidized by SAVAK (as were so many of the mullahs), Beheshti needed to protect himself by disposing of those who knew about his past. Together with some of the seculars who had a similar need because of their ties to the U.S. (Entezam, Minachi, etc.), he encouraged the creation of the Islamic tribunals and the idea of hasty trials. Beheshti succeeded in this and got Khomeini to appoint him President of the Supreme Court, which gave him the power to appoint judges at his own discretion. After hearing the accusations made against our regime, everyone expected a long public trial of its officials. There was nothing of the kind. Accused of "corruption on earth" (an expression from the Koran), members of our government were judged in secret and shot without delay.

The archives of the offices of the President of the Council, the Minister of Defense, the Minister of the Interior and the SAVAK were seized by Beheshti and his men. At our embassy in Washington, Yazdil's son-in-law announced the existence of documents showing the payments of bribes to important officials. When asked for details, he said the documents had been sent to Tehran. There, his father-in-law said the documents had been lost.

From the first weeks, all witnesses and documents which could have compromised those in power (through their past associations with the Shah or foreign powers) or shed some light on how this religious revolution came about, disappeared. It would have been embarrassing, to say the least, if, in the heated climate of those early months, it were widely known that Beheshti had close ties with SAVAK, that Chamran occupied high military posts in the PLO, that foreign Minister Ghotzbadeh represented Arafat in Paris and that Yazdi was an American citizen.

Of those four men, three are dead: Beheshti murdered, Chamran killed in an airplane "accident," Ghotzbadeh shot by firing squad. Yazdi, thrown out of the government, now lives in seclusion.

In the second phase of his revolution, the creation of a theocratic state under his personal control, Khomeini no longer needed his former allies. Using Beheshti's Islamic Republican Party, Khomeini began to eliminate the seculars. Of this Party, Sheikh Tehrani would say: "It's another SAVAK with a more significant budget. There is also more corruption. The party has its own prisons and frequently used torture ... The heads of the Party resort to repressive techniques to impose their domination."[81]

Beginning on August 8, 1979, Khomeini denounced the opposition, which "organizing strike on top of strike, lie after lie, is seeking to weaken the Islamic Republic." (I found a certain irony in this—for one year ago Khomeini's supporters helped destroy the Shah's regime in exactly the same way.) Immediately, the Procurer General outlawed several newspapers and arrested their editors. The Revolutionary Guards searched the homes of other members of the press and took them away without warrants. The party named after Shariat-Madari and the National Front run by Matine-Daftary, Mossadegh's grandson, protested. Shortly thereafter, these two groups were dissolved. Shariat-Madari was placed under house arrest and Matine-Daftary fled to escape certain execution.

Khomeini was now ready to impose on Iran a constitution based on his own political ideas. Six months before, when he returned to Iran, Khomeini had made promises of a different kind: "The provisional government's first task is to organize the election of a representative Assembly that will prepare the referendum for the Islamic Republic and plan the Constitutional Charter for this Republic. Every Iranian Muslim's religious duty is to participate in this vote."[82] Now, on August 18th, Khomeini had this to say: "Those who insist on the necessity of a constitutional assembly in truth act against Islam. If our revolution, like so many others, had decapitated thousands of these corrupt people or burned them a the stake at the very beginning, this problem would not exist today." Two months later, in the midst of tightening repression, he threatened the discontented: "I am reminding you for the last time: Abstain from having meetings, from making criticisms, from circulating communiques. If not, I will break your teeth."[83]

It was in this climate of repression and execution that Khomeini's constitution, written by his mullahs, was born, after a referendum organized by Beheshti and his Pasdarans. The central concept of this document is that of theologian-guide, the Vellayate Faghih, developed by Khomeini during his exile. Once the power of the Faghih is established, any insurrection or revolt becomes sacrilege—and therefore punishable by death. There is no division of power. The executive, the legislature and the judiciary are all subject to the supreme authority of the Faghih or his appointees, the Assembly of Faghihs. Judicial authority depends on the Faghih. Since the Faghih is the guide for all, including any accused, there is no need for a defense in any judicial proceedings. The citizen's duty under this constitution: Total obedience to the decisions of the Guide. His position: Eternal minor, since he cannot ask the government, which is responsible only to God, to account for itself. Contradictions abound in this document. For example, the first article states that the Republic is founded on the will of the people as expressed in the referendum. But the second says that the Republic is based on faith in Islam and on the capability of the Faghih. Article 56 declares that Allah, the absolute sovereign, has accorded full sovereignty to humanity in the determination of its social organization. But the capability of the Faghihs, which is based on the Koran and tradition is permanent—and therefore supplants the sovereignty of the people. In short, this constitution follows the line of any form of orthodoxy: Submit to the leader or risk being banished from society (in this case from the earth and the hereafter). Such absolutism cannot allow differences, which would rupture the entire structure.

To understand what this Islamic Republic is, we can begin with a glance at the regime's budgets: The office of Religious Affairs is allocated double the amount given to external or cultural affairs. Its funds are fourteen times greater than those of the Ministry of Work and Social Services. Next we can see that the mullahs of the Republican Party have declared three groups of citizens to be enemies of the state: intellectuals (leftists or westernized people); nationalists (Kurds and others); and democrats (supporters of a multi-party system). On the basis of this thinking, the mullahs began a kind of Islamic cultural revolution. They purged the bureaucracy of all non-Islamic elements. The criterion for the recruitment of officials became knowledge of the Koran, rather than any technical ability. Universities were closed in order to "Islamicize" professors and textbooks.

HUMAN RIGHTS: Since the Shah was pulled down on the issue of human rights, I feel it urgent to point out that the permanent suspension of such rights is inherent in the present regime, as it was in Hitler's fascist regime. There are, in fact, several striking points of similarity, as American journalist Fergus Bordewich points out:[84]

> "The ayatollahs have given their cachet to a different kind of racism by translating the notion of spiritual purity onto the political plane. In their ideology, foreign customs are not merely different or challenging: they are poisoned cultures, they are 'sick'... secular education does not have simple shortcomings: It 'injects poisons into the people's minds and ethics.' In this climate, the racist impulse can be turned against anyone who can be accused of being 'western influenced.' Anyone with unusual ideas or habits can be the carrier of 'disease.' Leftists, liberals, intellectuals and artists, for example, could all be tossed eventually into the same category as prostitutes and homosexuals, whom the government has

methodically persecuted for 'corruption.' How nauseatingly familiar it all sounds. Heinrich Class, head of the Pan-German League and one of Hitler's mentors, wrote in 1912: 'So-called humanity can be re-established once we have been reformed politically, morally and hygienically.' Thirty years afterward, amid the extermination of the Jews, the pupil declared proudly: 'The battle in which we are engaged today is the same sort as the battle waged during the last century by Pasteur and Koch. The Iranian reactionaries, like the Nazis, have depersonalized their opposition. In the logic of racism, it seems simply wise and healthy to wipe out dangerous 'bacteria.' If your finger suffers from gangrene, what do you do?' The Ayatollah Khomeini asked Oriana Fallaci.' 'Do you let the whole hand and the body become filled with gangrene, or do you cut the finger off?' With cool logic, he added: 'We want to implement a policy to purify society.' The government of the ayatollahs has at the very least established an intellectual and 'spiritual' rationale for political repression."

Real power in a fascist regime is situated above the institutional power, as it is now in Iran. A second characteristic is the use of terror as a means of government. On this point, I will quote a document published by Amnesty International on January 2, 1982: "The entire country lives in an atmosphere of fear. The revolutionary guards search homes at all hours of the day and night and arrest arbitrarily whomever they want. The people are now seeing the sad truth: An old mullah on his prayer rug is ruling the country with much more brutality than the King of Kings on his throne ever did."[85]

After all those hundreds of articles on repression during my brother's regime, it is useful to take a fresh look at one: "Repression in Iran continues to grow heavier. Added to the nine terrorists accused of having murdered three American officers and executed on January 24th, one of whom was a young woman, two others were tortured on Monday, February 2nd. Their case will be tried before the military courts, as any crime involving unlicensed weapons comes under their jurisdiction."[86] The same paper published in the second year of the Islamic Republic the following editorial, titled "Bloodbath in Tehran":

"The Islamic regime in Tehran celebrated the first anniversary of the war in the Gulf started by Iraq on September 22, 1980 in its own manner—with a veritable blood bath. The list of executions carried out on Friday and Saturday is particularly heavy and without precedent: 182 members of the opposition, most of the Mujahiddin, were summarily executed in the court of the sinister Evin Prison and other detention centers around the country. Among those executed were 81 youths, one person accused of having given medical supplies to the 'counter-revolutionaries,' Kurds, and a mullah known for his sympathy for the Mujahiddin ... Messieurs Guilani and Lajevardi, respectively judge and Revolutionary Procurer of Tehran explained Saturday ... that Islam permitted the 'immediate execution by firing squad of persons captured'... In fact the abusive references to the teachings of the Koran are merely a front designed to disguise their cold determination to drown all opposition to their regime in blood."[87]

Under such a regime, laughter and joy are gone, in their place an atmosphere of perpetual sadness. When a brave attempt is made to lighten the atmosphere—even an innocent childish one—it is brutally punished. Recently a friend told me of his sister's 16th birthday celebration—a group of young girls sharing a cake, some laughter and music. Without warning, a gang of Revolutionary Guards burst into the house, arrested the girls—and administered 20 lashes to each, for the crime of a few moments of frivolity. Travelers returning from the Islamic Republic tell many such stories. One said:

> "You can see the plain hatred for Khomeini in the eyes of the people who stand in line to buy bread. People don't need words to express their thoughts. You can see it in their eyes, in their demeanor, in the way they turn their faces away when they see a portrait of Khomeini or hear his voice on the radio.
>
> "The people associate Khomeini with repression, misery, unemployment, poverty and a total lack of security. Let me tell you what the people say. They say: 'Before we would go to the mosque to pray, to the university to study, to the stores to buy food, and to the cemeteries to mourn the dead. Now we go to the mosques to buy food, to the university to pray, and to the cemeteries to celebrate the holidays.' The Islamic regime has changed everything. Here's what the people say: 'Before we would go out and drink and come home to pray. Now it's just the opposite. I am 60 years old and I have seen many things in my life. But this regime is such that I would not wish it even upon my enemies to have to live there. Even under the Oajars, it must have been paradise (compared to this)."[88]

The New York Times, which had published so many anti-Shah articles, not to mention editorials anticipating the reasonable and moderate regime Khomeini would institute, recently recognized the condition to which my country has been reduced:

> "The UN has no time for Iran's crimes. A few months ago, an Iranian exile gave delegates a list of 7,746 names, most of them leftists slain by the ayatollahs' firing squads. No one would sponsor a resolution. Third world nations

won't turn on a non-aligned partner; Europeans, West and East, find it expedient to avoid quarrels with Iran. "President Reagan has done the minimum by speaking out for the Bahais. Congress has passed a resolution. What speaks louder is the silence among so many who used to denounce the Shah as a tyrant and pleaded for patience when Ayatollah Khomeini replaced him five years ago."

"At that time, an article on the opposite page castigated the press for depicting the ayatollah as a fanatic. Princeton's Professor Richard Falk wrote that this, 'seems certainly and happily false. Indeed, the ayatollah may yet provide us with a desperately needed model of humane governance for a third-world country.'

"Iran is a dark place. Its economy is a shambles, its youth die in a holy war against Iraq. Its executioners are overworked, its despotic mullahs are ignorant of the world. But not too loud, please. Voices that might sway Iran—on the left and among the non-aligned need to become audible."[89]

A few days later, I noticed with interest the curious fashion in which Professor Falk attempted to dignify his embarrassment and to differentiate my brother's regime from Khomeini's:

"We have deplored these excesses as energetically as we earlier opposed those of the Shah. Three years ago we formed the Emergency Committee for the Defense of Human Rights and Democracy in Iran to express our continuing commitment to these concerns in the post-Shah period. The Committee has been active in various ways, including urging the UN Humans Rights commission and other international bodies to cast their light of censure upon these outrages.

"We must recognize one crucial difference between the circumstances of the Shah's rule and that of his theocratic successors. The U.S. played a prominent role in placing and keeping the Shah in power. Khomeini's reign, however grotesque, is a product of domestic ferment and struggle in Iran. In this respect, there exists less direct American leverage and responsibility.

"There is much for all of us to learn from this bitter experience in Iran. I can only say that the overwhelming majority of Iranians committed to human rights and democracy welcomed the revolution at the time as a deliverance from darkness.

"Khomeini's plans for post-Shah Iran were then obscure. He fooled and later persecuted, many dedicated, humane followers and may himself have moved by stages and for a variety of reasons to lead the Islamic Republic in such a demonic direction."[90]

8: THE HOSTAGE IMBROGLIO

THE HOSTAGE CRISIS: So many tens of thousands of words were written about those long, anxiety-filled months when America was "held hostage" by Khomeini's "students." They passed, unevaluated into history, until the facts leading up to the takeover came to light, through documents seized by the "students," and through the personal revelations of those who took part in the drama. This was a period I can never forget, for it was a time when I experienced, moment by moment, the pain and suffering of the man who was, since childhood, the very center of my life. I know I cannot expect others to share my personal feelings about the man who was the Shah of Iran. But I cannot and will not be silent about the appalling treatment he received at the hands of an administration which advertised its commitment to human rights so heavily, which used its particular interpretation of these values to undermine the government of a longtime ally.

If I can do nothing else, I must now lay to rest the fabrication that the Carter administration had no choice but to treat my brother as they did, that the Embassy takeover was precipitated by revolutionary fervor, by the indignation of Islamic "students" over the possibility that the Shah would be offered the simple humanity of asylum and medical treatment for a grave and terminal illness. I think it is clear now that my brother was used, quite effectively, as a means for consolidating the power of the mullahs. If my brother had mercifully died peacefully following his departure from Iran, I am certain that Khomeini would have found reason to generate a crisis involving the U.S., to reach his stated goal of bringing Iran's relations with the U.S. to zero as rapidly as possible.[91] With the information I now have at hand, it is possible to reconstruct the events leading up to the seizure of the Embassy, the intrigues that accompanied by brother's search for asylum, and the steps by which Khomeini divested himself of his secular allies.

Late in September of 1979: Time is running out for the Bazargan government. It is the last impediment to the total domination of Iran by the clergy. From his stronghold, the Islamic Republican Party, the Ayatollah Beheshti wages political battles on several fronts. Within the Revolutionary Council he must still contend with the demands of such civilian politicians as Bani-Sadr and Ghotzbadeh, for although Khomeini is committed to clerical supremacy, he still has use for these men and extends his protection to them. For Beheshti, an important priority is to separate the seculars from Khomeini, to create sufficient dissension to rupture the tenuous and temporary alliance as quickly as possible. Already he had managed to persuade Khomeini to institute the revolutionary tribunals, which he controls—rather than the extraordinary tribunals, under government control, as proposed by Bazargan. But his power is still limited. Chamran commands the Revolutionary Guards, while the middle classes and the leftists support Bazargan. Beheshti recalls a conversation with Hojatoleslam Khomeini, who described the Young Islamic students growing disenchantment with the present government. Beheshti sees in this disaffection an opportunity to undercut the Bazargan government and enhance his own power. Bazargan has been pushing for a normalization of relations with the U.S.—a position which makes him vulnerable. Beheshti decides to use the students, to fan their anti-American sentiments and use them against his enemies. He sends for Khomeini.

THE SHAH'S CONDITION DETERIORATES: After his stay in Egypt and Morocco, my brother arrived in the Bahamas. At this time, the U.S. had been giving repeated reassurances that he could come to New York for medical treatment whenever he chose to do so. Suddenly and without warning the Bahamian authorities refused to extend visas for my brother and his family. They were given ten days to leave. In his book *Answer to History*, my brother talked about this sudden shift: "I now have my own theories about their change in behavior. Then they were only vague suspicions as to why we were asked to leave. Although the casino interests are the financial mainstay of the Bahamas, British influence in this former territory has remained strong, as it has elsewhere in the Crown's colonies. I have a longstanding suspicion of British intent and British policy, which I have never found reason to alter. With the U.S. distant and cool, and the British, as always, hostile, Bahamian Prime Minister Piddling wanted me out ..." Two days before the visas expired, a Bahamian official contacted one of my brother's secretaries to ask if the Shah wished to remain. He refused, choosing to accept the invitation he had received from the Mexican government.

My brother's suffering, the strain of traveling from country to country, were compounded by the news from Iran. I watched his health and his spirits decline as he became a wandering spectator to the disintegration of all he had accomplished in his 37 year reign.

His condition worsened rapidly. Between August and September he lost about 20 pounds. He suffered from jaundice and a recurring fever. At first, Mexican doctors diagnosed his condition as malaria, but when their treatments proved ineffective, Dr. Benjamin Kean, a specialist in tropical ailments from New York Hospital, was called in. Dr. Kean disputed the diagnosis of malaria, and in the course of two consultations determined that my brother, who had become quite emaciated, was suffering from obstructive jaundice, hard tumor nodes in the neck and a swollen spleen—signs that his cancer had worsened. In addition, he had severe anemia and very low white blood counts.

In his own account of this time, Dr. Kean recalls his conversations with my brother: "I said, You must be hospitalized so that we can make the correct diagnosis. Almost certainly, you will need an operation. This is a very complicated case and you have multiple life-threatening illnesses. No one doctor can handle your case. You need a medical team—a diagnostician, surgeon, oncologist, hematologist, radiologist, nutritionist, infectious-disease specialist, and supportive house staff. You need a teaching hospital." The Shah said, 'Where can it be done?' We worked our way up. Slowly, I rattled off the countries with adequate facilities—North Africa, Britain, Brazil, Argentina. He just sat there and shook his head. 'I am not welcome.' I said that most properly he should return to France, whose physicians had been treating him all along. 'I am not welcome.' It all came down to U.S. or Mexico. The Shah was a proud man, and he was quietly bitter that his former ally of 37 years would not offer him a haven. His questions to me were always, 'If I were to come to the U.S., where should I go?' I mentioned Houston, Los Angeles, Palo Alto, San Francisco, Chicago, Boston, and, of course, New York. The Shah's medical and security advisers had checked out the best medical facilities in Mexico City and there were three reasons why he preferred the U.S. to Mexico: Security (the Shah feared assassination and Mexican facilities are notably lax), language barriers (only the top Mexican medical officials speak English and few of the Shah's advisers spoke Spanish), quality (there is no way the best Mexican facilities can match the best American)."[92]

Negotiations were underway to admit my brother to New York Hospital. In the midst of a growing anti-American climate in Tehran, the U.S. Embassy was against such a move. Henry Precht went to Tehran to advise Yazdi and Bazargan that the Shah would be arriving in New York. The two seculars were, of course, quite antagonistic to such a decision, since it would threaten their increasingly tenuous position in the mullahs' government.[93]

THE CRISIS ERUPTS: In Tehran, the fundamentalist students are impatient. The schools and universities are not yet closed, and they serve as gathering places for debates and discussions on the progress of the revolution. There is anger with the Bazargan government: The radical reforms promised in February have failed to materialize.

Why has the government delayed its implementation of Khomeini's ideas? Why are the factories still in the hands of their owners? Why has the crest of the old regime not been removed from official correspondence? Why are banknotes bearing the Shah's picture still in use? Why have the intellectuals not been arrested? And why is the sale of Western and Marxist publications still tolerated? Agents of Beheshtils IRP, and student followers of the extremist mullah Khomeini, fan the impatience and discontent. They charge members of Bazargan's government with being CIA agents, others with maintaining ties with "the great Satan America." This is not difficult, since four members of the Bazargan government carry American passports. "See how Yazdi came to the assistance of the American ambassador in March," was one accusation, referring to the first attempt to take the U.S. Embassy. "See Ghotzbadeh with his suit and tie and American ways ..."

Most damning of all was the Imam's reprimand to Bazargan, news of which spread quickly throughout the capital: "You are a weakling, Sir" (the "sir" meaning Americanized).

On October 22nd, news of my brother's admission to New York Hospital gives the new regime a powerful propaganda tool, to divert from its inability to restore order, or to run the county it has taken. It gives the students a cause to consolidate strength and support. "The illness is just an excuse!" they preach. "The Americans are preparing a coup against our revolution. We must do something—now!" A member of the student group later says: "It was a matter of the prestige of our country. Our honor was stained. We decided to make an action so that the cries of our oppressed people could reach all the world's ears and through the problem of the Shah, we wanted to show what America had done to the whole world with its international trickeries."[94]

At first the students plan was simply to blockade the Embassy, to remain there long enough to arrange a press conference which would have given them a forum to the world. They move on November 4th. With the complicity of the police forces, they occupy the Embassy, now rechristaned "the nest of spies." On Beheshti's advice, Khomeini sanctions this flagrant violation of international law and all conventions of diplomacy—which he dismisses as diabolical inventions of imperialism. He sends his son Ahmad to join the students, to demonstrate that they have his approval and protection.

For the old man an occasion is indeed a gift from Allah. It diverts attention from serious internal problems—the food services, the stoppage of all services, the unemployment, etc. "Make them return the Shah and the millions he stole," he preaches, striving to turn the crowds' hostility away from the government which cannot govern. His message is simple but effective: If America returns the Shah and his money, all of Iran's economic problems would be miraculously solved.

Khomeini has now successfully challenged America and, by extension, the hated West. Ten days after the taking of the hostages, he harangues the crowds: "Do not be afraid of the United States," which he described as a source of "nothing but evil." To reinforce the ayatollah's message, Iranian television broadcasts the speech, along with a film clip showing a foot crushing a package of Winston cigarettes.

For 444 days, from November 4, 1979, to January 20, 1981, the world saw a series of unprecedented events. The treatment of the hostages, which several of them would eloquently describe after their release, the sophisticated manner in which they were intimidated and abused would demonstrate that their captors were no ordinary university students, but rather trained terrorists. The government's stance would be a challenge to all traditional rules of order—a clear signal as to how the mullahs' movement would be conducting business in the future, how it would equalize its position by making its own rules.

From the beginning, Khomeini makes his position quite clear. In a full-page advertisement in the *New York Times*, he says:

> "Let me announce here that we are neither afraid of military interference nor are we afraid of economic siege, since we are Shi'ites and as Shi'ites we welcome any opportunity for sacrificing our blood. Our nation looks forward to an opportunity for self-sacrifice and martyrdom. Now let us suppose that in the absence of all reasoning, Mr. Carter or perhaps the superpowers should agree to send military forces here. Well then, we have a population of 35 million people, most of whom long for martyrdom. We will go to battle with all these 35 million people, and once we are all martyred, then our enemies can do whatever they want to with this country...
>
> "Again, as for economic siege, let me remind you that we are a nation who has long since been accustomed to starving ... If such should be the case we will all fast... We will continue growing wheat and barley in our own fields and the yields of the crops will be sufficient for us. Well, perhaps we will have meat only once a week—and incidentally it would be a wholesome diet to eat less meat—maybe we will have one meal a day."[95]

Gradual appeasement follows, though each concession is followed by new demands. The terrorists insist that America admit its "crimes" in Iran—and political minds from the White House to the UN try to find a way to satisfy these demands without inflicting intolerable offense to the pride and sensibilities of the American public. It is, of course, an attempt which fails, which costs Carter the next election, which earns for him the title of "rightful heir to the Neville Chamberlain."

Khomeini's domination of the world political scene won him the title of *Time Magazine's* "Man of the Year for 1980." Speaking to the West through the magazine, he demanded the extradition of my brother, arguing that the Shah was not admitted to the U.S. for humanitarian reasons, but abducted by the Americans to ensure that he would not divulge their secrets. He also insisted on compensatory damages and American repentance—suggesting that the Americans would also do well to get rid of Carter and elect a suitable president. When the demand for a public repentance is made, Carter will not say "no." He responds by saying he is ready to make an "expression of concern" regarding the U.S.'s past conduct in Iran. The jailers now add new demands: not only do they want an apology, they want the return of the Shah and all his possessions.

Carter's response is once again weak and equivocal: "I cannot turn the Shah over to you, but I will deport him, and then it is up to you to follow the matter up." So my brother is told he must leave the U.S. The international network that has helped put Khomeini in power pursues my brother, cutting off other possibilities of asylum. Mexican students demonstrate against his admission to their country, and Mexico withdraws its offer of a haven. Naively, or at least for public consumption, Carter's government accepts the explanation that the students had occupied the Embassy because of the Shah's admission to New York hospital. Later, it will be seen as the bold political maneuver it was —and questions will be asked. Why, when it was known that there would be trouble of some kind, when the State Department had been alerted to the vulnerability of the Embassy—why had the old ayatollah been left such a strong card to play (not only the Embassy, but also twelve volumes of highly sensitive diplomatic communications—not shredded, as was popularly reported*, for in fact very little of this material had actually

---

* In a lecture at Columbia University attended by several former Iranian diplomats, Sullivan revealed that these documents had been sent to the State Department during the turmoil of early 1979. The documents were returned to the embassy in Tehran after Bazargan became prime minister, perhaps because the State Department mistakenly felt secure with the new government. Sullivan added (to the amusement of the audience): "I wish the documents had been sent instead to Columbia University. Then they would have been lost forever!"

reached the shredder)? One which would consolidate his power and ensure his survival? Later, Hamilton Jordan would give the only kind of answer a Carter spokesman could give: "We felt it was important to have representation on the ground in Iran. We knew it was a risk. Obviously, in hindsight, we were wrong."[96]

Carter sends my brother to Lackland Air Force Base, near San Antonio to wait. One by one, the countries where my brother had planned to seek asylum withdrew their offers. I flew to Lackland to be with him, to seek comfort as much as to give it, for I was still in shock following the assassination of my son Shahriar. The weather was cold and rainy and harsh, the barracks that were yet another stop in the long and painful search for a place to rest were spartan and tightly secured. My brother's health was failing rapidly, but he was as always, dignified and uncomplaining, trying to give strength and assurance to us, his family.

We talked for long hours, about the past and present, about our country, and about the sorry spectacle we were seeing at the time, of the futility of trying to appease the "holy man" who ruled by terror. I felt such bitterness at the turning of people like Kurt Waldheim, who had suggested that charges against my brother be tried before an international commission; and Anthony Parsons (the same man who had urged my brother to rapidly institute free elections, saying: "Even if you lose your throne, you will go down in history as a leader who remained faithful to his democratic ideals."), who in his new post at the UN, invited Khomeini's envoys to air their grievances before the Security Council.

My bitterness would grow in the weeks to come, as my dying brother would be held hostage himself, as the Carter people would break promise after promise. While we were at Lackland, Hamilton Jordan and Lloyd Cutler, special adviser to the White House, arrived to discuss plans for my brother's transfer to the Panamanian Island of Contadora. They assured him that he would have access to Gorgas Hospital in the former American Canal Zone, a facility which was equipped for the treatment of cancer. They added that in the event of a medical emergency, he could always return to New York. The point was made that since Panama had no diplomatic relations with Iran, there would be no fear of antagonizing Khomeini here. Before my brother flew out to Contadora, Carter telephoned and wished him a speedy recovery, and to repeat the reassurances given by his envoys.

The first weeks of his stay on Contadora passed uneventfully. During this period Kurt Waldheim sent a mission to Tehran. Headed by the Algerian Ambassador to the UN, this group was to investigate the crimes of the U.S. and the Shah. The mission failed because the "students" refused to allow the delegates to see the hostages. However, Ghotzbadeh used the occasion to air more propaganda. Just as he did with Waldheim, he produced a parade of SAVAK "victims," maimed and mutilated people—and no one questioned where and how these people had been disabled (later, one of the regime's organizers fled to France and spoke of how he had "rented" the services of the crippled and sick for such occasions). Khomeini's next move was to ask the government of Panama to arrest the Shah. My brother learned from friends that the local authorities were negotiating with emissaries from Tehran. Torrijos denied the rumors which began to spread. But by the beginning of February 1980, the Minister of Foreign Affairs declared that my brother was virtually a prisoner, since he could not leave the island without permission from the government. In fact, the authorities had increased the number of guards surrounding his villa. We heard more alarming reports coming from Washington, regarding secret negotiations between Carter and Khomeini. Despite official denials all around, the Panamanians continued their talks with Tehran, as did Carter (using two "adventurers," a description he gives in his memoirs). It was at this time that Hamilton Jordan flew to Paris to meet Ghotzbadeh, who advised the assassination of my brother as a "solution."

My brother's condition had dramatically worsened. An immediate operation to remove his spleen was necessary. The Panamanians refused to allow the surgery at Gorgas Hospital and insisted the Shah go to the local hospital instead. My brother had no choice but to accept. When his surgeon, Dr. Michael DeBakey, arrived in Panama on March 14th, he was refused permission to enter the hospital. Carter's men reneged on all their former reassurances and refused to intervene in any way that would assure my brother decent medical treatment.

I was beyond disbelief, and it was only slightly reassuring to know that my disgust was shared by many Americans: As columnist George Will expressed it: "To appease the terrorists, the Administration betrayed American values by deporting an old ailing ally to a fly-blown island in the tropics. Enough is known about disease to know that psychological factors can have physical consequences; the 'will to live' matters. If people wanted to weaken the Shah's will, they could hardly do anything meaner than to banish him to the malicious custody of Panama's General Omar Torrijos, a dictator who escaped Carter's censure."[97]

The Shah returned to Contadora, and once again our old friend Anwar Sadat courageously invited my brother to come to Egypt. Carter immediately sent Lloyd Cutler to warn my brother that his presence in Egypt would harm Sadat's position in the Arab world, and that his transfer to an American hospital would negatively affect the negotiations for the release of the hostages. Cutler added that my brother could have the operation in Gorgas Hospital.

None of us had reason any longer to trust any communications issued from the White House. I called President Sadat myself and told him that my brother was reluctant to impose on an old friend or to jeopardize his political position. This courageous and truly religious man repeated his invitation and said that he would not take "no" for an answer, adding that "a guest is a gift from God." My brother flew out of Contadora two days before he was to have been arrested by the Panamanians and delivered over to Khomeini. The President's men, however, were not yet finished with him. His plane was stopped in the Azores on the instructions of Hamilton Jordan. Mercifully my brother arrived in Egypt. When his spleen was removed, it was grotesquely swollen 20 times the normal size. His cancer had reached his liver, and we were told that he would die within a few months. My brother believed that the time of death was preordained. I do not share his view. I believe that his life was cut short; but at least he spent his last months under the protection of a faithful friend.

RESOLUTION: After my brother's departure from Panama, the hostage crisis was no nearer a solution than it had been before. An editorial in the *Washington Star* summed up the opinion of the time:

> "In hindsight, which is often unpleasantly clear, the U.S. would have done better from the outset to take a strong line on its right to extend further medical asylum to the Shah—to have said to the Iranians, in strong language, that our standards of asylum would not be dictated from Tehran and that any harm to the hostages would be severely punished...
>
> "Unfortunately, our policy of conciliation, having compromised fundamental principles, has been perceived as a policy of weakness. So regarded, it has in fact *become* a policy of weakness. Yet the hostages are not free and little has been accomplished but to provoke embarrassing expression by the Shah of his lack of confidence in our good faith, our good offices, and our will to protect him from humiliation and death."[98]

In March 1980, President Carter addressed a letter to Khomeini, which was published in Tehran. The President complained that he had "inherited" a foreign policy which "led us to commit errors in the past." It cited Nicaragua and Chile, as well as Iran, and described the ability of a democracy to "condemn its mistakes." It spoke of a "commission of inquiry" in the American Congress and of "a great effort to give the Iranian people the necessary satisfaction." Finally, the text has Mr. Carter saying: "I can very well understand that the takeover of our country's embassy in your country could have appeared to you as the understandable reaction of Iranian youth." The White House disavowed the published version of the letter, but in a somewhat equivocal manner. The *Wall Street Journal* had this to say:

> "The notion that there must be at least some substance behind the text is proving hard to squelch. And on reflection, what lends the notion credence is the administration's past handling of the crisis. It has salami-sliced itself into each 'next step' held out by the Iranians; we have all been mentally preparing ourselves for its eventual abject apology to the Iranians for the inconvenience of their having to seize our hostages.
>
> "We are no longer astonished by any humiliation the administration will accept in the name of the hostages, but even after all of this, we are astonished that grown men are proposing to enlist in the same game. The Senate Foreign Relations Committee is contemplating issuing its own white paper on our relations with Iran—becoming a commission of inquiry to condemn the past errors of U.S. policy in order to give satisfaction to the Iranian people, exactly according to the text of the letter released by the Iranians ...
>
> "What is at stake in Iran is not merely the hostages, who have not been helped by Mr. Carter's policies, but the perception of the American position in the world. With each American humiliation, there is new reason for other Persian Gulf states to seek what accommodations they can find with revolutionaries, religious fanatics, and the Soviet Union."[99]

I suspect that it may have been former Attorney General Ramsey Clark who suggested such a letter to President Carter. It was Clark who wrote to Ibrahim Yazdi in October 1979, advising on the best course of action against the Shah, proposing a series of legal actions to extradite my brother and transfer his personal fortune. The President had sent Clark to Iran in the first days of the crisis, but Khomeini had refused to see him. However, Clark did participate in the "International Conference on the American Interventions in Iran," which was organized by Ghotzbadeh and Bani-Sadr and held in Tehran from June 2-5. In his opening speech, Khomeini said: "Our nation is counting on you who have come to Iran to recognize the crimes of the United States and the dethroned Shah, and it is waiting for justice and fairness from you. We hope that the results of this inquiry will be the censure of the oppressor." When Ramsey Clark took the floor, he acknowledged his country's "crimes," and when he had finished, he knelt before the delegates to "beg their pardon" in the name of the American people.

Shortly after Clark confessed to crimes in the names of America, the Public Broadcasting System aired a two-hour documentary entitled: "Iran: Inside the Islamic Republic." This film portrayed my brother's reign as repressive and Khomeini's Iran as a model of freedom, democracy and human rights. The credits attributed the financing of the film to a "branch of PBS," together with Iranian investors. Among the listed producers were a number of Khomeini's diplomats, who had been expelled by the U.S. I found it rather curious that a public television channel receiving government subsidies would broadcast such a film at a time when American citizens were being imprisoned and tortured by Khomeini's students.

I will not take it on myself to analyze the reasons behind the Carter administration's mishandling of the hostage crisis, but I cannot resist speculating that the internal conflict vis-a-vis my brother's regime still prevailed, now taking on a "who lost Iran" quality. When I read that Henry Precht had been named to head the State Department task force, I had no doubt that the President would be encouraged to accept Tehran's demands regarding my brother. I believe it was the NSC group which engineered the aborted military rescue. This, like the secret negotiations with Ghotzbadeh, had the effect of strengthening Khomeini's regime and endowing it with a great deal of prestige. He had defied the most powerful nation on earth and proved to his Muslim neighbors that Allah was on his side.

It was Khomeini who decided when and how the crisis should be resolved—at a time when the political value of the hostages had been fully exploited, and when the cost of continuing to hold them might prove far too high. When he found himself facing a new American President, one who had made clear his intention to take decisive measures, Khomeini accepted the Algerian mediation which brought the episode to a close (proclaiming: "Did I not say that Carter would not be re-elected? Allah is with me."

The crisis had served him well, for it enabled the mullahs to take bold action against the "seculars" who polluted their revolution. On the 25th occasion of Algerian independence, Bazargan and Yazdi attended—and met with Brzezinski, who represented the U.S. This gave Beheshti the "proof" he needed that the seculars were traitors, working in collusion with the "great spy" Brzezinski. The Bazargan government was forced to resign, and power passed into the hands of the clergy. Only Bani-Sadr and Ghotzbadeh, Khomeini's personal proteges, were left, isolated among the turbaned heads, powerless to voice any dissent or opposition in a violently anti-western climate. After the signing of the Algiers agreement, the Iranian negotiator, Behzad Nabavi, gave an interview to the newspaper *Kayhan*, revealing just how successful his government had been:

> "The U.S., which had been pushed out the door, was trying to return via the window. The interim government was trying to improve relations with the U.S. The internal social situation was bad and the society was becoming ungovernable... [The crisis] had achieved its goals. These were the fall of the interim government, ending internal chaos, the disarming of the leftists, counter revolutionary and hypocrite (Mujahedeen) groups, the exposing of

all the multinational characters and finally, all the political and economic results which led to a move toward self-sufficiency and the breaking of ties with U.S."[100]

The American view of the crisis summed up by A.M. Rosenthal, executive editor of the *New York Times*:

"We mourned because there was a feeling in this country until the 444th day that it was not just the 52, but all Americans and, worse still, our very government that had been taken captive and held hostage in that embassy ... That was part of the American character revealed: Compassion for the victim. But that compassion could not extend to the leader taken prisoner."[101]

9: LIFE IN THE ISLAMIC REPUBLIC—HOLY TERROR AT HOME AND ABROAD

IRAN UNDER KHOMEINI: United Nations, New York, October 5, 1981. It is the 36th session of the General Assembly. Before this body where I spent many productive years, Khomeini's Foreign Minister, Mir Hussein Musavi Khamenei, delivers a speech, which covers his government's position on human rights:

> "Our people view these advocates of human rights whose hands are drenched in the blood of the oppressed people throughout the world with the contempt and derision they deserve. We are quite familiar with the nature and the sort of human rights that the United States of American advocates. This is the sort of human rights that keeps silent when Yankee imperialism commits mass murders throughout the world but suddenly becomes vociferous when the murderers of the president, prime minister and scores of others in Iran receive their punishments in our revolutionary courts. This is the sort of respect for human rights that does not move a hair to condemn the

military apparatus of the Zionist non-entity when it mass murders the innocent people of South Lebanon ... We declare unequivocally that we have no faith in the sort of human rights whose advocates are recruited from among the American and European capitalists, world Zionists or notorious racists."

Qasr Prison, near Tehran, February, 1981. It is eleven o'clock at night, and Syavosh Bashiri, a former newspaper publisher during my brother's regime, is asleep in a tiny cell crowded with other prisoners. Suddenly the door clangs open and an armed guard calls out: "Your turn has come." Bashiri weeps as he is dragged into the courtyard where six other prisoners are already lined up against a stone wall. Some of the men cry and plead for their lives, as the firing squad takes aim. There is a burst of machine gunfire, and six men fall dead. Bashiri is covered with blood, but he is still alive. The guards take the man, who is trembling and nearly out of his mind with terror, and throw him back into his cell. The Ayatollah Khalkhali, the IRP's "hanging judge" has ordered the mock execution in order to break Bashiri's will. Six months later, after having released his worldly possessions to the judges, Bashiri is released, thanks to the intervention of a senior member of the prison staff, a man who was repelled by Khomeini's justice.

In the summer of 1981, Bashiri slipped over the Iranian border into Turkey, and then went on to Paris. There he was interviewed by an English journalist, who told his story:

"Bashiri paid the mullahs vast sums of hush money. In all he handed over 175,000 pounds in Iranian currency, most of it borrowed from friends. But his generosity only seemed to make them more greedy, and when they had squeezed him dry, the mullahs had him arrested and put into Ghasr.

"In Ghasr the word of Ayatollah Khalhkali is law ... According to Bashiri, Khalkhali's day at Ghasr begins at two in the afternoon. He spends the mornings attending the Majlis, the Iranian parliament, where he is a member ... (after his one hour siesta) he gets down to the serious business of the day—judging the dozens of prisoners who have been rounded up in swoops the night before. There is the usual mixture of thieves, homosexuals, prostitutes and drug addicts to cope with. The political prisoners he saves for later.

"Prisoners are paraded before him in batches of twenty. Passing sentences takes only a few minutes ... There is no appeal. Anyone with the temerity to protest that his sentence is too harsh has it doubled automatically. Once, Bashiri recalled, Khalkhali was suddenly summoned to a meeting with Ayatollah Khomeini. He had no time to deal with the prisoners, so he decided to sentence the occupants of the first prison bus to three years, the second to five and the third to seven. Many prisoners are in addition ordered to be tied to a concrete bench and lashed with electric cables. The women, their legs covered by jute sacks in the cause of Islamic modesty, are hit with rubber hoses."

"Towards five o'clock, Khalkhali, a short bearded man, starts his tour of the political prisoners' cells. Snapping his fingers, he moves briskly among them, selecting victims seemingly at random: 'You there, you've had it,' he says. 'Outside.' Not a trace of emotion shows in face.

"The condemned men are embraced by other prisoners and taken away swiftly to write their wills. But if these include substantial bequest of money to their families, they may find that they are temporarily reprieved. The next day they are taken under guard to their banks and forced to withdraw all their savings. Only then are they shot, while the money is handed over to Khalkhali for safekeeping ... Khalkhali has enriched himself with his victims' money ..."[102]

New York, January 1983. Zia Nassry, an Afghan-born American citizen, has just returned from Iran, after spending 966 days in seven of Khomeini's prisons. He was seized in his hotel room; blindfolded, interrogated for a day, declared guilty of espionage and sabotage, and ordered shot. After his release he described his experience to the *New York Times*.

> " ... They tied me up on a pole. They opened fire. They fired from very close range, maybe three meters ... I could feel gun powder or the wind of the bullet going past. At first I thought I had been hit. A minute or two later they shouted: 'Bring that so-and-so here' ... There were (in Evin prison in October 1980) maybe 3000 prisoners, mostly members of the old cosmopolitan elite ... After the Iran-Iraq War broke out the number jumped to 25,000. A new wing was built and prisoners were living in burned-out buses brought to the prison..."

The *Times* article added:

> "Mr. Nassry said that though there had been beatings and executions all along, the level of brutality increased after March 1981, following a riot ... on the night of June 19th, he said, he saw trailer trucks arrive in the prison courtyard bringing hundreds and hundreds of blindfolded men and women. Some were beaten as they waited. The population of his own cell on Ward I rose from 14 to 95... According to his account, some inmates were taken and summarily shot. They were mostly young people ... He had been able to count 233 bodies being loaded on trucks from the prison hospital..."[103]

These stories are by no means unusual. As early as February 1980, the international secretariat of Amnesty International published a report on "Law and Human Rights in the Islamic Republic of Iran"[104] It concluded that "the legal procedures employed by the courts are such that the accused persons have not received fair trials, that the charges upon which they have been arrested are often extremely broad and that sentences of death have been frequently passed ... Islamic revolutionary tribunals posses jurisdiction over, 'anti-revolutionary' and 'counter revolutionary' offences. Broadly speaking the former category may be understood to encompass activities directly or indirectly in support of the Shah; the latter refers somewhat more specifically to activities directed or perceived to be directed against the Islamic Republic. In the case of 'anti-revolutionary offences' criminal liability may be based only on participation in the 'illegal' governments of the Shah." In another section, the report recognizes that "arrests carried out by Komiteh personnel without proper authorization or by persons unconnected with the Khomitehs were commonplace." The report further notes that "The indictments make reference not only to secular offences, but also to religious concepts of Islamic Law such as 'mischief through the land'" (commonly referred to in English as 'corruption on earth'). This is taken from Sura 5, verse 33 of the Koran, which reveals that "The punishment of those who wage war against God and his apostle, and strive with might and mane for mischief through the land, is: Execution or crucifixion, or the cutting off of hands and feet from opposite sides, or exiled from the land. That is their disgrace in this world, and a heavy punishment is theirs in the hereafter."

In 1981 and 1982, AI reported a worsening of the situation: "Many former prisoners interviewed by Amnesty International described specific ill-treatment of prisoners, in particular of prisoners being whipped while suspended by their wrists and the beating of the soles of the feet. Other methods of torture reported to Amnesty International included burning with cigarettes, burning with iron and mock executions. Some informants said the torture started as early as May 1979. Some described the torture of relatives in order to induce people to give themselves up or to intimidate the family as a whole. In other cases tortured prisoners were shown to families so that the families would persuade the prisoners to confess to avoid further torture. In many cases people have died under torture and their deaths have subsequently been announced as executions."[105]

"Tehran's prisons are now so overcrowded that new blocks are hastily being built and new locations being found ... Those in Iran's jails today have no idea why they have been arrested. They could have been rounded up for 'looking' at the scene of a blast, for reading a political pamphlet, for condemning the regime on a tapped telephone, or for arguing with a neighbor who reported them ... The regime has publicly urged teachers to report on students, students on teachers, landlords on tenants, tenants on landlords, neighbor on neighbor. Khomeini himself has often called on the entire nation to 'spy' on one another. In such an atmosphere, human jealousies often lead an innocent to jail ... Iran's revolutionary courts and jail staffs refuse information on many captives to relatives or friends seeking their whereabouts. It is difficult to estimate, or even guess, how many missing there are in Iran at any given time ... Qasr cannot be described as a prison but as something less than a stable. There are 6,000 persons packed into space originally planned for 1,500. There are many people inside who have been waiting months for some official to tell them when they might be tried. There were several who had been waiting two years ... health conditions are not observed at all."[106] No improvement was reported by AI in 1983 or 1984, and in fact the 1983 report describes a new torture variation employed in a Komiteh prison, where "about 40 children ages 1 to 12 years are lodged because they are the authorities' trump card for obtaining confessions ... 'When the mother is whipped, the child is led in to look at her.'[107] A policy of severe repression and intimidation requires a solid secret apparatus for implementation. Shortly after Khomeini returned to Iran, his Palestinian advisers reorganized the remnants of SAVAK and created SAVAMA, which is now considered to be one of the most fearsome and ruthless secret policies in the world, with the authority to kill at random and at will. Its first chief was Mustafa Chamran. After his death, reportedly it was taken over by Hossein Fardoust and Kave, a former SAVAK official.

Among those who have suffered most at Khomeini's hands are Iran's intellectuals, often men and women who had studied in the West—and who had been quite critical of the Shah for not introducing western liberalism and western values quickly enough. Many of these people supported Khomeini's revolution, though I cannot imagine how they believed a clerical government would allow them even a fraction of the freedom of expression they enjoyed during the Shah's regime. Those who were not fortunate enough to flee the country have suffered the kind of experiences described by British Mid-East specialist Edward Mortimer in the *London Times*:

"... One report based on details compiled by friends and acquaintances concerned the death of Omid Gharib, an intellectual who studied in France since 1973, and returned to Iran after the revolution. He was arrested on June 9, 1980. He had written a letter to a friend in France, describing the situation in Iran and the policies of Ayatollahs Khomeini and Beheshti's Islamic Republican Party. The letter was opened. Omid's house was surrounded by revolutionary guards who entered it by force and ransacked it. He was taken away and his books and journals were confiscated ... (after months of detention) he was sentenced to 3 years imprisonment. During the 20 months of his imprisonment he was transferred many times from one prison to another and on several occasions he was beaten and tortured ... He was transferred in June 1981 to Qezel Hessar prison where he was held for 8 months without being allowed a single family visit. On February 10, 1982 his parents learned that their son had been killed two days before. They were told that they could go to fetch his will, but were turned away empty-handed.

"Information available indicates that between 70 and 80 people are held in cells about 19 ft. square, so that prisoners have to take turns to sleep. Food is scant and bad and permissions to use the lavatories is severely limited. Whippings and other torture such as burning with cigarettes and irons and the pulling of fingernails are so common that they have become an integral part of the prison routine.

"Things are far worse than under the old regime. To avoid publicity the Savak torturers tried not to kill their victims. Ayatollah Khomeini's henchmen have no time for such niceties. Tortured prisoners are often left alone to die and some are killed by attaching an instrument that inhibits breathing. In such cases, the pretense of judicial death is maintained and bullets are shot into the bodies. Nor does a death sentence bring relief. A member of parliament who often visits prisons orders revolutionary guards to rape women before they are shot, so that 'they might be denied the slightest chance of entering paradise.' Recently documents show that those about to be killed have had blood taken, to be sent to the front in the war with Iraq."[108]

The point I want to make here is not that my brother's regime was less horrible than that of Khomeini's, for that would hardly be a matter of pride—but that it was fundamentally different. The Shah was the ruler of a Middle Eastern country, not a western one, and there were elements in his government which could be considered undesirable to western eyes. But my brother was a reasonable man whose ideal was to make our country a model for the region. Although he felt (rightfully, I think) that Amnesty International and similar groups had singled out Iran for an intense campaign that was out of all proportion to conditions which prevailed, he received their representatives in a civilized fashion, allowed them to make their inspections and invited their recommendations. Throughout the country, he fundamentally altered the quality of life. I have before me a letter written to the Shah by William J. Butler, chairman of the executive committee of the International Commission of Jurists (a man who most certainly was not an admirer of my brother's). In it, he wrote:

"The world has watched with great interest the significant steps taken by Iran toward the implementation of many of the principles described in the International Covenant on Economic, social and Cultural Rights was ratified by Iran on June 24, 1975.

"We have noted with interest the substantial improvement in such areas as land reform, health, housing, agrarian betterment, literacy and more specifically, in the field of women's rights. The redistribution of land in thousands of villages to many thousands of Iranian citizens, the dramatic increase in life expectancy, the dramatic increase in literacy, together with the education and placement of women in all branches of the Iranian society are most impressive accomplishments and we are delighted to see that these trends continue."[109]

When I read or hear comments to the effect that Khomeini's Iran is worse than the Shah's Iran, I realize that these miss the point. Of course, conditions in all areas are worse, but more important, they are radically different. Except for those who believe in the rewards of martyrdom, Iran's people today are without hope and without joy. Under my brother's regime, certain rights were taken for granted, among them:

- The right to a minimum standard of living
- The right to enjoy the fruits of lawfully earned property
- The right to education
- The right to employment
- The right to privacy and the sanctity and inviolability of the individual's home
- The right to choose a personal lifestyle
- The right to travel freely in Iran and abroad
- The right to freedom of religion

All of these rights have been systematically breached on a massive scale—and not in a random manner. The revocation of these rights is not a post-revolutionary condition, but an integral part of the socioeconomic framework envisaged by the mullahs. In a speech delivered in the early months of his regime, Khomeini proclaimed: "We did not make a revolution to eat chelokebab (a popular Iranian dish) ... Even donkeys eat grass ... No, our aim was to instill real Islam." A supporter of Khomeini's revolution described life under Khomeini's brand of Islam in a letter to the *Wall Street Journal*:

> "Khomeini said that the Shah was importing everything from other countries and that our exports were next to nothing. You should see us now. Six million of our work force are unemployed. Our foreign reserves have dropped from approximately 12 billion to 1.5 billion dollars. We have a war that takes away one third of our daily budget, a war provoked by Khomeini when he sent his mullahs to Iraq to make speeches to export his rotten revolution. Thanks to Khomeini we have two million homeless people ... there is a substantial shortage of all foodstuffs. There are long lines for eggs, meat, chicken, milk, yogurt, rice, sugar, washing powder, cooking oil and soap ... Our universities are still closed ...
>
> "All we hear are empty slogans, such as 'death to imperialism.' But our chicken is imported from France through Libya ... The same goes for many other goods. We hear the slogan 'death to America,' but recently business has started with American firms.
>
> "We are living in disaster land; we are living in a state of permanent terror; we are alive but not living. You can see that by looking at the faces of the people walking in the streets. They seem to be in a daze. In the morning we wake up to the sound of the radio announcing new executions ...
>
> "In certain government organizations and companies, secretaries and bosses cannot directly contact each other. A special male agent carries messages between them. Women cannot go to parks without a head scarf, let alone to restaurants, government offices, supermarkets. Men hairdressers, if found out, are whipped for

touching women's hair. This life style is normal in Saudi
Arabia because there it has always been like that. But it
doesn't make sense here. You can only make a nation
go backward by force, and the funny thing is that
Khomeini was condemning the Shah's father for having
removed the veil by force. Well, Khomeini put it back on
by force."[110]

A man who held several senior positions in the Khomeini
government before he was ousted in 1981 has since made a
number of secret trips to Iran. After his last visit, he told *Time
Magazine*:

"When I went to Iran three months ago, I thought the
situation could not get any worse. I was wrong. The ruling clergy have turned Iran into one huge funeral parlor.
Death and the related ceremonies are the only diversion
available. A thick miasma of repression and gloom has
settled on the land."

"In Urumieh, located in northwest Iran, all one sees
are soldiers, Islamic guards veiled women and sallow-
faced apprehensive men and children. The city, once
among the cleanest and most picturesque in Iran, is now
an eyesore; a panorama of uncollected garbage, decaying
public works, empty shops and people in tattered
clothes."

"In several other cities, I saw enough to conclude
that the Khomeini regime is under siege."[111]

Impressions of western journalists are not significantly different. In the Spring of 1982, Khomeini allowed the return of a
number of foreign correspondents, in order to show them the
war atrocities committed by the Iraqis. John Kifner of *The New
York Times* recorded these images:

"Powerful mullahs riding in bullet proof Mercedes limou-
sines with smoked windows, followed by carloads of

armed guards. Fifteen year old boys volunteering to walk across Iraqi mine fields. Long lines forming before six o'clock in the morning for scarce rationed food. Political graffiti scrawled on walls around the city: Death to women whose heads are uncovered. These are some of the sharpest images of a return to revolutionary Iran after an absence of fifteen months."[112]

From Elaine Sciolino of *Newsweek*:

"For all its fervor the military parade marking the third anniversary of Iran's Islamic revolution recalled only faintly the tumultuous February day in 1979 when the closed truck inching through a million jubilant Iranians carried Ayatollah Ruhollah Khomeini into Tehran. I witnessed both celebrations ... These days everyone talks of the executions under Khomeini. 'When I look at my address book, nine of ten people have either been arrested or executed,' says one friend. The market place is ruled by chaotic food lines and the extortion of the economic underground. Social cohesion is sustained largely by suspicion and hatred ... Iran's anti-Americanism has hardened ... Says one diplomat: 'They search our mail. They break into our houses. They terrify us. We're all wondering who's next.' The diplomats are not alone ... Iran's Islamic society is far-from-happy model of reform ... A middle-class friend asked: 'When are the Americans coming back? Please tell me that there will be military action to save us ...' One friend, arrested for his work with an American company, was locked in a windowless cell for twenty days and beaten. Parents spoke bitterly of a son who went shopping, found himself caught in a street brawl and was arrested and executed ... At home the shortages have forced strict rationing of meat, chicken, eggs, milk, cooking oil, butter, gasoline, kerosene and other essentials ... Revolutionary leaders have incorporated the shortages into their creed. As a Parliament speaker puts it: 'Too much wealth brings recklessness and misery.' But wealth still does as wealth can. Fifty cents buys an egg on Tehran's black market, and ten dollars buys a chicken."[113]

Norms of behavior have been defined by the mullahs in their published "Guide for the Perfect Muslim," which instructs Iranians not to miss any of the five daily prayers, not to entertain, to limit their sleep in order to read the Koran, to dress simply, etc. Imperfect Muslims know that these instructions are no longer a matter of personal conscience: Unfaithful wives are stoned to death; liquor consumers are whipped; petty thieves have their limbs cut off.

On its way to instilling "real Islam," the new regime began by dismantling my brother's modernization projects. It stopped the construction of dams, nuclear plants for generating electricity, roads, housing projects, new factories, etc. It nullified land reform and replaced it with an "Islamic land reform," an idea which has yet to be implemented. Running inflation gnaws away at the income of those who have work. Food staples are increasingly scarce, pharmaceutical drugs lacking. Endemic diseases such as malaria and smallpox, which had been eradicated during my brother's reign, are reappearing. Censorship is universal. The press is under the mullah's control; films are cut; passages in books and magazines are suppressed, to eliminate scenes and photographs not conforming to Islam. In January 1984, two Australian diplomats were expelled for "insulting the principles of Islam"—because they had required female visa applicants to be photographed unveiled.

The universities, which were closed since 1979, are just beginning to reopen. However, most previously offered courses of study are banned. The recruiting of new professors is based not on competence or credentials, but on knowledge of Islam. Potential students must fill out questionnaires requiring detailed information on their families and past activities, as well as their hobbies, preferred pastimes and their views on the "future of the Islamic Republic." To their applications, they must attach a

drawing of the layout of their homes. A notice reminds applicants that all "incorrect answers" will be dealt with by punitive
measures. Revolutionary Guards inspect homes at all hours of
the day or night, to determine if lodgers are conforming to Islamic norms. They open and censor letters.

Women have lost all the rights acquired through long years
of hard work. This is particularly painful for me, since I have
spent much of my life trying to improve the condition of women
in Iran. Our women, who were among the most emancipated
in the area, were able to enter Parliament and occupy ministe-
rial positions. Today they are denied access to administrative and
liberal professions. Those who dare to appear unveiled or "im-
modestly" dressed are subject to brutal mistreatment. (In Saudi
Arabia, where women have traditionally been covered, an offender might risk spray paint on the offending parts; in
Khomeini's Iran, an unveiled face invites the throwing of acid).
On July 25, 1984 the IRP let loose in the streets 20,000 hoodlums screaming "death to those who do not respect the Islamic
code of dress." The obsession with the "Islamic code of dress"
has reached absurd proportions. In 1980 the mullahs ordered
the banks not to change French bills of one hundred francs. The
reason: one side of the bill bears the portrait of Eugene
Delacroix, the other an engraving of his most popular painting,
"Freedom"—a woman with bare breasts. While excesses like this
are almost laughable, the treatment of Iran's women is heart-
breaking. I do not think there is a country in the world today
which systematically terrorizes its female population as
Khomeini's Iran does:

Akram, a young office employee: "I was waiting in line for
a bus to take me to work. Suddenly a man approached and
threw acid in my face. People around me were screaming. I was
screaming because the pain in my eyes was awful. The bus driver
took me to a hospital. They refused to admit me because they
were afraid of the Komiteh. This happened in two more places.
Finally, I was accepted in the fourth hospital, which lacked
medicine."

Chahla, a young middle-class woman: "Without any reason
I was thrown in jail, in a small dark, stinking room with a dozen

other women. I was beaten with fists and thrown down on a sort of straw mat. There was no convenience in the cell. We had to eat and relieve ourselves in the same place. One day I committed the imprudence of telling the other women I would allow my son to make his own choice of religious and political conviction. The guards dragged me down to the cellars and enclosed me in a jute bag. I was hit more than fifty times with water hoses. Later they put me on a chair and tied my hands behind my back. One of the torturers who answered to the name of Ruhollah said to me: 'You know, female, you must cooperate with us, for we also know how to be kind.' He was a brute with an unshaven face. He unbuttoned his trousers while the others untied me. I was raped by all three."

Fatmeh, a member of the Mujahiddin: "At Evin Prison almost all the girls have been raped, but to the guards' way of thinking, it was not rape, for there is no harm in raping girls who will not go to paradise. As for torture, they never say the word. They talk of punishment, and their consciences are at ease. Me, I was whipped. I knew little girls who were executed and parents who were put to death in front of their children."

United Nations, New York, November 18, 1982. At the 37th session of the General Assembly, the representative of the Netherlands spoke at the official reunion of the Third Committee, concerning the report submitted by Iran to the Human Rights Committee:

"It was with the greatest anxiety that his government (the Netherlands) had followed the Iranian government's continuous and massive violation of the most fundamental human rights and freedoms, which were unconditionally and unambiguously safeguarded in the Covenant. The Human Rights Committee's consideration of the report of Iran not only revealed a contempt for the members of the Committee on the part of the representative of Iran, but also disclosed that country's disregard for international law and for universally accepted human rights norms. It was tragic to see a State submit that in fact it no longer recognized the primacy of international law. Having taken note of the numerous reliable reports on the situation in Iran, he (the

Netherlands representative) wondered what provisions of the Convention were still being upheld by a government which engaged in arbitrary arrests and detentions, torture and arbitrary and summary executions, even of young children. Such wanton destruction of human life and dignity was extremely difficult, if not impossible, to reconcile even remotely with the spirit or the letter of the Covenant. The Human Rights Committee, quite rightly, had not even tried to do so."[114]

Not everyone suffers in Iran. Those with means buy the services of smugglers and escape through Turkey. Those with greater means buy exit visas (currently selling for about $30,000) from Islamic government employees, which allow them to leave on regularly scheduled flights. The clergy, of course, suffer not at all. The Hojatolislam Muhammad Montazeri's son, Ayatollah Montazeri (Khomeini's designated heir) has appropriated millions of dollars for himself, in the name of "Islamic Organizations of Liberation" abroad. The mullah nicknamed "Ringo" (who was assassinated during the June 1981 blast which destroyed Islamic Party headquarters) deposited millions of dollars in Swiss banks. The Ayatollah Beheshti, killed in the same blast, had received $22 million in commissions on the purchases of arms, which he also deposited in a Swiss account. It is ironic that these mullahs, who had preached for so long against the monarchy's disrespect for human rights and its corruption, now confiscate properties for their own use, traffic in food products, foreign exchange, the sale of caviar, the export of fraudulent antiquities, etc.[115] To be sure, Khomeini has tried, without much success, to curb his mullahs' interest in wordily goods. In one of his more coherent speeches, he said:

"Certain Imams and mullahs provoke the disaffection of the population due to their undue interference in governmental affairs and high taste for luxuries ... If the people abandon their confidence in the clergy, this signifies that it is condemned to failure ... When buildings, cars, and objects of luxury proliferate in the hands of the religious, the result is detrimental to Islam. I am preoccupied with this problem and I do not see how to solve it. By their love for luxury, the religious give ground to

those who affirm that 'religious despotism' governs the county
... Such a behavior weakens the government and pushes the
people to detest the religious."[116]

INTERNAL DISINTEGRATION: During the 50 years of Pahlavi
reign, our national unity and territorial integrity was re-
established twice, once following the first World War, and once
again after World War II. Iran's national unity began to crumble
shortly after Khomeini's return to Tehran. Within a few weeks
autonomist movements began in Baluchistan, Kurdistan and
Khuzistan. In Kurdistan, we have a full scale civil war that has
dragged on for five years, resulting in large scale destruction and
thousands of dead. Khomeini has refused to negotiate with the
Kurdish leaders. Instead, he has launched both regular army
forces and the Pasdarans against the Kurds, massacring men,
women and children, without discrimination. Any prisoners
taken are executed for "counter-revolutionary" activities. In
Azerbaijan, the Naqshbandi, a Sunnite tribe, carry out regular
raids against Khomeini's troops. In Baluchistan, the rebels control a number of important towns, which no longer recognize
the Tehran government. In the Fars province, the Ghashgais defy
Khomeini's authority, despite the hanging of their tribal leader
in 1982. In the northeast, the Khazai tribes carry on regular
skirmishes with the Revolutionary Guards. In several regions, the
central government has been obliged to relinquish authority to
the rebels, because it simply does not have the manpower to
wage war on so many fronts.

THE WAR WITH IRAQ: Since September 1980, Iran has been
engaged in what one French journalist called the "forgotten
war." It is the longest war between two countries since World
War II, though it rarely receives widespread press coverage
unless supertankers are destroyed. It has cost more than 400,000
dead and wounded on our side and displaced more than 2
million Iranians. Monthly, the dollar cost of the war runs between 500 million and one billion. The result was a deficit in
1983 of billions of dollars. In his vendetta against the govern-

ment of Saddam Hussein, Khomeini is willing not only to martyr the entire country, but also to sacrifice its future generations.
In February 1984, the *New York Times* correspondent described
battlefield scenes never before seen in the civilized world:

> "Their ticket to paradise is the blood-red headband and
> the small key they wear in the battle ... (they are) young
> boys aged 12 to 17 recruited by local clergy or simply
> rounded up in the villages of Iran ... and sent weapon-
> less into battle against Iraqi armor. Often bound in
> groups of 20 by ropes to prevent the fainthearted from
> deserting, they hurl themselves on barbed wire or march
> into Iraqi mine fields ... Across the back of their khaki
> colored shirts is stenciled the slogan: 'I have the special
> permission of the Imam to enter heaven'... an East Eu-
> ropean journalist who witnesses one of these
> human-wave assaults ... could hardly believe what he was
> seeing, as first one boy, and then another, detonated a
> mine and was hurled into the air by the explosion. 'We
> have so few tanks,' explained an Iranian officer to the
> journalist without apology.
>
> "Five years after the revolution that toppled the late
> Shah Mohamad Reza Pahlevi (sic) and led to the totali-
> tarian theocracy of the Ayatollah Khomeini, Iran seems
> a society possessed ...[117]

From a correspondent for French television, describing the
war from the Iraqi side and published in *Le Monde*:

> "What upset us more than the thousands of dead we had
> seen the day after, was the arrival of prisoners, directly
> from the battle. There were dozens and dozens of stu-
> pefied, bone-tired children, bleeding, covered with blood
> and dust. One of them, eyes covered, hands tied behind
> his back, waited to be interrogated. He was nine years
> old ... The general who commanded the battle told us
> he had the impression of having witnessed a mass ex-

ecution. It was exactly our impression ... At the entrance of what remains of the village of Beida, one literally walks on carpets of corpses. In the face of such butchery, what strikes one first is not how they could have killed all these children, but who is mad, beyond all imagination, to have ordered such an operation? ... These twenty thousand children or adolescents fought in swamps against a trained army ... the real Iranian army was behind the children and did not move.

"Khomeini has no sympathy for any of the children captured by the Iraqis or for other Iranian prisoners. He flatly rules out any exchange of prisoners. He scolds: 'I don't consider the prisoners of war to be true Muslims. They escaped. They did not go to martyrdom.'"[118]

If Khomeini has no sympathy for our own captured children it is not surprising that his treatment of Iraqi prisoners of war was found less than humane by a delegation of the International Red Cross. The delegation was expelled (summer, 1984) after it reported general mistreatment, torture, brainwashing and wanton killing of Iraqi prisoners.

From an editorial in the *New York Times*, of May 22, 1984: "In Henry Kissinger's apt phrase, the ultimate American interest in the war between Iran and Iraq is that both should lose. The underlying hope is that mutual exhaustion might rid the Middle East of the aggressive regimes of both Ayatollah Khomeini and Saddam Hussein, yet leave their nations intact to avoid a superpower rush into the vacuum ..."

February 1984, Isfahan. Iran's second largest city marked the fifth anniversary of Khomeini's rule—with a public celebration of what the mayor called "a monument more wonderful than Persepolis." It was a vast graveyard with the capacity for a million tombs. Twenty thousand of these places have already been filled, most with young boys.

JIHAD: THE EXPORT OF REVOLUTION: Tehran, October 10, 1979. Khomeini addresses pilgrims en route to Mecca, repeating a now familiar theme: "We cannot tolerate any longer these kinglets, sheikhdoms, and monarchies which reject true Islam. We must create new organizations. We must export our Islamic revolution."

Mecca, November 20, 1979. In the gray light of dawn, pilgrims from all corners of the world fill the great court of the mosque which houses the Kaaba. The faithful perform their ablutions, in preparation for the first prayer of the day. Some carry coffins, bringing their dead for a last prayer in the shadow of the sacred Black Stone. Suddenly a loud wailing cry is heard: "I am the Mahdi (Messiah)!" A bearded young man dressed in white robes, cries out again: "I am the Mahdi!"

Scattered throughout the crowd, about a hundred men rise and point to the young man, chanting in unison: "Yes, he is the Mahdi ... the Mahdi has arrived." While the "Mahdi" holds the crowd's attention, his "followers" open the coffins, arm themselves with machine guns and station themselves at all exits. Within a few minutes, the pilgrims and the shrine are taken hostage. The following day, another group of this Mahdi's partisans attempt to take over the great mosque of Medina, where the prophet is buried. This time the Saudi army is prepared for the attempt and quickly crushes the intruders.

Crown Prince Fahd dispatches a tank, which breaks down the great doors of the Mecca mosque and secures the courtyard. The terrorists take refuge in the hallways, where they have grouped their hostages. The army hesitates, for conventional assault methods might destroy the sacred relics. Prince Fahd appeals to the French. They send in a team of specialists who quickly penetrate the mosque, kill the "Mahdi" and round up the surviving rebels, who will be quickly tried and executed. Khomeini's first attempt at Jihad has failed.

News of this does not surprise me: The domestic situation in Iran is deteriorating daily. The old ayatollah has been obliged to dismiss his secular Director for Petroleum Affairs, along with a number of technicians, because they refused to carry out their five daily prayers, saying "The Koran cannot solve matters pertaining to oil wells and refineries." Inflation is rampant, unemployment is on the rise, rebel insurrections tax the resources of a country already drained by the way with Iraq. The failure in Saudi Arabia can be a setback for Khomeini, a sign that Allah no longer supports him. Neatly, he proclaims that the young man who led the insurgents was a false prophet, an agent of the Americans and the Zionists who wish to discredit the Islamic Republic.

Moscow echoes his disclaimer. Its information services announce that the "great Satan" America had organized the mosque takeover, generating a wave of anti-Americanism in the Muslim world. In Pakistan, crowds attack and set fire to the American Embassy. Later, some interesting facts come to light when Mehdi Baratzadeh, the Charge d'Affaires of the Islamic Embassy in Sana, defects. Baratzadeh reveals that following instructions from Tehran, he recruited 59 young Yemenis from an Iranian training camp, provided them with arms received through the diplomatic pouch, and directed them to Saudi Arabia, shortly before the mosque takeover. Among leaders of the Islamic countries, an "alert" condition prevails. Time and time again, Khomeini will demonstrate that his call for Jihad is not merely an effective tool for rallying the masses in Iran; it is in fact a fundamental pillar of his regime, as stated in the preamble to his Islamic constitution: "... Considering the content of the Islamic revolution, which is a movement for the victory of the weak against the powerful, this constitutional law creates the basis for the continuation of this revolution outside as well as inside the county, and most particularly in the domain of international relations. In cooperation with other Islamic movements, it endeavors to pave the way towards the creation of an Islamic nation, united and global ..."

These are not the idle ravings of an old man with fantasies of regional and global domination. The dangers he poses are both real and immediate. He has both the will and the means to spread his revolution. The myth of the savior-messiah, inherited from Zoroastrianism, is at the core of Iranian Shi'ism. The coming of the twelfth Imam, who will re-establish peace and justice had been foretold and in Iran it is a fundamental part of the collective and consciousness. Endowing himself with the mantle of the savior messiah, Khomeini has successfully politicized Islam. He is an inspirational (and dangerous) example to every dispossessed and ambitious faction which can call itself "Islamic" in nature. His speeches, geared to the illiterate and politically unsophisticated masses, are simple, popular and compelling. To them he offers the promise of Paradise, the opportunity to challenge and destroy his enemies (by extension, enemies of Allah), the "heretic" leaders who are designated "corruptors on earth," "agents of imperialism"

Throughout the Middle East, Khomeinism grows and spreads. In Iraq, the Hojatolislam Muhammad Bagher Hakim (today in Tehran, where he presides over the Organization of the Islamic Revolution of Iraq), attempts to mobilize the Shi'ite community. The operation fails: the ayatollahs of the holy cities of Najaf and Karbela do not support Khomeini, and the authorities take swift and decisive action against Hakim and his followers. In Saudi Arabia, troubles in the Shi'ite communities near the oil fields of Ras Tanura lead the authorities to make conciliatory gestures (in the form of improved living conditions). In spite of the aborted attempts at Mecca and Medina, Saudi Arabia remains a high priority target for Khomeini. In the summer of 1982, the ayatollah assigns the Hojatolislam Muhammad Mussavi Khoeniha the task of generating agitation among the two million pilgrims assembled in Mecca. The Iranian Embassy in Riadh secretly prints inflammatory tracts, calling the masses to rise against the royal house of Saud.

Montazeri (Khomeini's designated heir) sends delegates in 1983 to a conference of Shi'ite opponents of the Saudi regime held in Cyprus.[119] In the Gulf region, Khomeini creates an "Islamic Front for the Liberation of Bahrain" (which has an important Shi'ite community) and sends a terrorist unit to Manama, the capitol. They are to begin sabotage actions which would facilitate the invasion of Bahrain by an armada of Iranian Hovercraft launched from the port of Bushire. The objective is to establish an Islamic republic. The operation is scheduled for December 16, 1981, the anniversary of Bahrain's independence, an occasion that would enable the terrorists to take important hostages from among the invited guests (these included King Khalid of Saudi Arabia). The government of Bahrain successfully foils the operation and arrests the plotters on December 13th. Once again, Khomeini denies participation. But the Bahrain authorities publicly display the seized arms and the pamphlets calling for a general revolt.

"The Islamic Front for the Liberation of Bahrain" registers a protest at the UN, against the "torture" perpetrated on its imprisoned members in Bahrain. The Hojatolislam Hashem Rafsanjani, president of Khomeini's parliament, adds:

> "Instead of throwing into prison some poor people, the Arab nations would do better by being united. If they were to close, in unison, the oil valves even for two days against America, the latter would never dare help Israel again. Instead Sheikh Yamani (the Saudi oil minister) decides to bring down the price of oil and makes a formidable Christmas gift, not only to the United States, but also to France and Japan."[120]

The invasion of Lebanon by Israel creates an opportunity for further activity in that country. Montazeri sends to Lebanon (via Syria) his best-trained Pasdarans, under the leadership of Khahani and Moayeri. But when the moderate Shi'ite Sheikh Shamsedinne Badrane refuses to accept them into the Amal movement led by Nabih Berri, the Iranians join a dissident Amal group (led by Mussavi) in Baalbek. The atyatollah's agents utilize fundamentalist sentiments everywhere, as a mobilizing force. In Algiers, Cairo, Aleppo, Tunis, leaflets are circulated describing the "eleven impure things" (urine, excrement, sperm, bones, blood, dogs, pork, infidel men and women, beer and the sweat of a garbage-eating camel). Female students begin to wear the veil, young men grow beards.

In Syria, the fundamentalists demand the revival of an old decree, forbidding women to go to the cinema. In Cairo, the students of the Al-Azhar, the Islamic university, call for the "return to Islam" and the "recovery of the Islamic republics of the USSR and the reconquest of Andalusia." The activities and the influence of the Muslim Brotherhood are revived everywhere. Fallen politicians, like Ben Bella, the former Algerian president, attempt to use Islam to bring down existing regimes.

Tehran, February 1984. On the occasion of the fifth anniversary of Khomeini's return, Hofatolislam Hashemi Rafsanjani, speaker of the parliament, announces that the revolution has been a complete success: The clergy occupy all important positions; women are forced to wear the veil; alcoholic beverages are forbidden; performing arts and music have been eliminated; Shari's has been re-established; the Koran is the principal textbook in schools and universities. "Today, Iran is the only true Islamic country," he says. Reporting on the occasion, a Tehran editorial asks: "Well, where do we go from here?"[121] The answer, of course, is: To other countries. A multitude of Khomeini's agents and imitators have launched operations abroad.

Algeria, November 3, 1982. A fundamentalist-inspired riot at the campus of Ben-Aknoun University results in one death and many wounded.

Algeria, February 6, 1983. Following fundamentalist-inspire disorders, the Algerian government denounces "external ramifications manipulated by foreign hands eager to destabilize the country, and groups abusively claiming themselves to be Islamic, in order to amass arms and bombs for the purpose of escalating violence."

Tehran, February 20, 1983. A young Algerian revolutionary, Rachid Ben Issa, visits Iran's capitol. In an interview with *Jomhouriye Esiami*, the government newspaper, he declares:

"The Iranian revolution has created a change more radical than the Russian or Chinese revolutions. For it is not consecrated to men, but to God. Men die, but God, He will never die.

"I call upon my Iranian brothers to be patient. I tell them: You are working on the scale of a full generation. You who live in Iran do not realize what you have accomplished. In the near future you will reap the harvest of your effort in the entire world. Be patient. You have students everywhere. Wait for them to complete their studies at the revolutionary school of your country. The day will come when Iran will be everywhere. Your revolution does not limit itself to a single county."

Kuwait, December 1983. American, French and (for the first time) Kuwaiti installations are the target of simultaneous bombings. The casualties are six dead and sixty three wounded.

Manilla, Philippines, December 2, 1983. A time bomb wrapped in Iranian newspapers is planted at the U.S. Embassy.

Bangkok, Thailand, December 3, 1983. A bomb explodes outside the Israeli Embassy, another near the former Iraqi consulate. Police believe these attacks were the work of Iranians.

Morocco, January 22, 1984. King Hassan II states that the bloody riots of the preceding days in the cities of Nador, Al Hoceina and Tetouan, were directed from abroad and "especially Iran." In his televised address to the nation, the King showed seditious leaflets bearing Khomeini's picture, impounded in Marrakech.

Jakarta, Indonesia, March 22, 1984. A group calling itself Islamic Jihad sends a letter threatening to attack installations and kill citizens of the U.S., Britain, France and Italy, in retribution for those countries' involvement in Lebanon. "Murder for murder," the letter says. "Allah is with us ... From now on, neither you nor your wives and children will find peace on Muslim soil."

Kuala Lumpur, Malaysia, March 24, 1984. Authorities lodge an official complaint about the distribution, by the Iranian Embassy, of leaflets preaching Islamic revolution and advising students to overthrow the monarchy. Later that year (September 1984), Malaysia's Deputy Foreign Minister bluntly informs an envoy from Tehran that he considered the activities of Islamic groups in Malaysia to be direct interference by the Iranian government.

Leaflets bearing Khomeini's picture are printed by Iranian Embassies and distributed to villagers in India, Pakistan,

Bangladesh, to the Muslim minorities of Thailand and the Philippines. Trained Iranians spearhead the formation of Muslim activist groups in these countries. Radical students are recruited and sent to training camps in Iran. Reporting on these activities, William Branigin of the *Washington Post* writes:

"Southeast Asia's moderate governments are becoming increasingly concerned about elements of Islamic radicalism from the Middle-East taking hold in the region. From Indonesia—the world's most populous Islamic country—and Malaysia, where Muslim fundamentalist groups trouble the government, to the Philippines and Thailand, with separatist rebels amid their Muslim minorities, the finger is pointed at Ayatollah Ruhollah Khomeini's stated goal of exporting Islamic revolution."

Tehran, Summer 1981. Khomeini's stated goals include the West, as well as the East. The Iranian Foreign Ministry organizes a seminar for its diplomats posted in western Europe. The agenda included the following items:

- How to export revolution and expand the scope of related activities within Europe and among immigrant workers.
- The study of internal contradictions within European states and movements of opposition.
- Coordination of Islamic propaganda in Europe. Actions against Iranian counter-revolutionaries exiled in European cities.
- Coordination of information gathering activities.
- How to influence the press and other channels of information in western countries.

Following the twelve-day seminar, Khomeini's "diplomats" return to their respective posts, to implement their instructions. Their agents infiltrate the ranks of Muslim workers in Europe, particularly those from North Africa.

France, April 1983. A report from the French secret service, the Direction de la Surveillance du Territoire (DST), describes the results of these activities:

"With a Muslim community of more than 2 million—the largest in western Europe—France could do little but help awaken the interest of Iranian fundamentalists ...

"In order to bring to fruition its policy in France, Iran has toiled to establish a clandestine organization, centered around its Paris embassy. It manipulates an important network constituted either by individuals or by cultural associations, whose official religious activities in fact mask their subversive activities.

"Embryonic at first, this network was minutely structured and covers today, if not the entire country, at least all the regions where sufficiently important Muslim communities are found. One can consider the organization which has been set up as 'operational' and ready to act ...

"By its intermediaries, and notably the abusive use of the diplomatic pouch, an important quantity of books, reviews, pamphlets, leaflets, magazines, is entering France. This propaganda is printed in Tehran by the official Ministry of Islamic Propaganda.

"It appears that Iran is trying, in a first stage, to utilize in France the increasing number of Muslims converted to fundamentalism through the activities of its subversive network, as means of politico-economic pressure, capable of serving Iranian interest, thus forcing our country to alter its policy. Two facts support this hypothesis: A few months ago, clandestine Iranian propaganda circulating in the gathering places (clubs) of immigrant workers or in the mosques attacked the social, economic, and fiscal policy of the President, as well as his international 'pro-Zionist and anti-Arab' policy.

"Evidently this campaign is orchestrated in such a way as to mold the mass of immigrant Muslim workers into systematic opposition, capable of materializing in demonstrations and strikes. This manipulation of immigrant workers on behalf of fundamentalist interests seems to have manifested itself for the first time on the occasion of recent conflicts in the automobile industry.

"Thus in the Renault, Citroen and Talbot automobile factories, it was clearly observed that the more intransigent immigrant workers on strike were backed by the Muslim Brotherhood. In the Peugot factory, the religious aspect of the disorders clearly appeared in the strikes, when workers recited religious incantations, brandished Islamic banners and demanded a place for prayers.

"Prior to these events, many workers from these enterprises (in majority Moroccans) had gone, for periods of 'formation,' to Iran. It appeared that the determination and the will of the Maghrebian leaders were so strong that the CGT (a French union), unable to control the masses, was obliged to incorporate some of them in their service of order.

"Other information on hand speaks of the growing concern of some French industrialists facing Islamic fundamentalist agitation in their establishments. They observe that the actions of certain fanaticized elements calling themselves the 'conscripts of God' meet with growing approval and are echoed among their coreligionists.

"This Khomeinist enterprise is cause for concern. If it continues to spread, it is feared that the majority of Muslim workers, obeying the 'Islamic" call, would be able to disorganize entire sections of our economy. If these conditions were to materialize, it would become an efficient means of blackmail for Iran."[122]

In Germany, a similar situation exists. Fundamentalism is being spread among Muslim workers, particularly those of Turkish origin. The Bonn government, which enjoys good commercial relations with Tehran, takes a lenient view of these activities. In return, it is said that Khomeini's agents have agreed to avoid acts of violence on German territory. These agents utilize Germany as a base of operations for activities in western Europe and the United States. (Understandably the German Foreign Minister returns from a visit to Tehran in 1984 with a recommendation that the U.S. re-establish relations with the ayatollah.)

Yugoslavia, March 1983. Yugoslavian cities with Muslim communities are flooded with Khomeini leaflets. Arrests are made on charges of "religious intolerance and the promotion of national hatred, as well as contact with foreigners." Later, *Le Monde* reports:

"Islamic extremists, visible under the influence of the integrist movement initiated by Khomeini worldwide, are beginning to agitate. They dream, according to *Illustrovana Politika*, of the creation of a vast Islamic state bordering the Mediterranean, which will encompass Yugoslavian territories, including Bosnia, from which 'nonbelievers' should decamp. Meanwhile, they attempt to make of Bosnia-Herzegovinia, a purely Islamic country, and are offended by the close ties between Muslims and non-Muslims, which constitutes a menace to the 'purity' of their religion..."[123]

In the U.S. and Canada, Khomeini continues his policy of ideological agitation, particularly among Muslim university students. Like Quaddafi, he offers substantial financial support to Islamic student organizations, which can be effectively used as political instruments. Like Quaddafi, Khomeini has also infiltrated black organizations which have some basis in Islam. (See *New York Times* editorial on Louis Farrakhan and "The Qaddafi Connection" in appendix).

Tehran, September 14, 1984. Hojatolislam Ali Khamenei, President of the Islamic Republic announces, at a prayer meeting, that he has formed a committee to "safeguard" the rights of black Americans. He adds that one of the aims of this com-

mittee was to "bring the United States to trial," and calls for the
creation of an international group to give support.[124]

January, 1985. Iranian Prime Minister Mir Hossein Mussavi
visits Nicaragua and Cuba. As the *Washington Post* says: "One
should not forget that Mussavi is the kingpin in Iranian terrorist activities and may be seeking to introduce in South America
activities used in the Middle East.[125]

I still find it inconceivable that the west ignores the nature
and the extent of the danger that Khomeini poses, that in some
circles there is still talk of "accommodation." In the *New York
Times*, for instance, I read an article proposing that the United
States should work "for a unified, stable Iran under the mullahs."
And the author added: "The west must be patient. We should
make a commitment to Iran's territorial integrity and develop a
wide range of political and economic contacts."[126] This suggests
that relations with Tehran can somehow be normalized, in the
western sense. Much more realistic, I think, is the certainty that
"normalization," with the establishment of diplomatic and commercial bases in the host country, will only facilitate the export
of Khomeinism into that country.

From the first days of his republic, Khomeini established
an agency for the implementation of his stated goals: The Department of Islamic Liberation organizations (headed today by
Mehdi Hashemi) within the Ministry of Foreign Affairs. However,
"Islamic Liberation" is of such importance to Khomeini that in
fact decision-making in this area is left to his heir-designate,
Montazeri. Abroad, Iran's diplomatic missions serve as bases for
revolutionary activities. These particular activities are coordi-
nated from Tehran, by Hussein Karimi, previous chief of the
Secretariat (under Prime Minister Mussavi). A special budget
(allocated through the Ministry of Foreign Affairs) provides the
embassies with funds and equipment for the printing and distribution of propaganda, etc. Through consistent abuse of the
diplomatic pouch, Iran's missions distribute not only inflammatory and seditious material against the host county, but also
arms, to be used in revolutionary activity and political assassination. (For example, in 1983, Montazeri attempted to organize

an "Islamic coup" in Turkey, under the cover of the Islamic Consulate in Istanbul.) They provide asylum, new "covers" and reassignment for agents on the run.

Reliable first hand sources have informed me that the West German embassy and the Rome-Athens-Cyprus triangle special-ize in this kind of operation (with the Rome and Athens embassies being specially equipped and secretly funded). When an agent is expelled or is forced to flee from Kuwait or Iraq, he goes to Cyprus, where Iran's "diplomats" provide necessary documentation and funds and reassign him to Syria or Algeria. Similarly, Iranian terrorists on the run from western Europe go to Cyprus or Athens, where they receive reassignment. Equally important in Khomeini's "Islamic Liberation" movement is the network of mosques, which operates under the control of Fadel Marandi in Tehran. These Shi'ite mosques recruit Islamic "fight-ers" and coordinate revolutionary activities with the embassies. Often, their directors are given diplomatic posts, so they may enjoy the benefits of diplomatic immunity.

Tehran, May 6–15, 1984. Montazeri holds a conference of the Imams of all the Shi'ite mosques of the world. Hundreds of participants gather, from the Islamic countries, England, France, Germany, Belgium, New Zealand, Nicaragua, Chile, the U.S., etc. The central theme on the agenda is: "How to Unify the Diverse Branches of Islam and How to Start an Islamic Revolution." Khomeini receives the delegates, whom he describes as "activ-ists of the word," and offers the following direction: "Do not wait to take power in order to speak. Speak until you have taken power ... In your speeches you must emphasize political and social problems. You must arouse the masses against imperial-ism, despotism and atheism. It is for you in your prayers to arouse the people against their governments. If they attack you, I am certain that the people will react and defend you. And this is what we want." Working closely with the mosques are the schools (for Islamic or Persian language studies), cultural asso-ciations and Islamic students' associations. Instructors and directors for these organizations are handpicked for intensive training in specialized schools in Qum and Tehran, which are generally run by Palestinians.

France, January 1984. Many of these subversive "cultural" establishments have been shut down, their personnel considered personae non grata. Journalist Duran-Souffland writes:

"... These professional propagandists are believed to be as persuasive as they are active, notably within the immigrant Muslim communities. Utilizing simple language, highly appropriate for an audience with generally little education, these dispensers of good words know how to convince ... In addition to speeches, fundamentalist agents have important material means ... From multi-directional export of revolution by means of religious intoxication towards the Jihad, and from Jihad to murderous terrorism, there is only one step. We already know that this step has been taken, and that intellectual terrorism can bring forth another, the one which blindly kills."[127] The "muscle" for the "Islamic Liberation" movement is provided by brigades of thugs, under the direction of Colonel Fassihi, formerly of SAVAK, currently of SAVAMA.

London, January 16, 1985. The *London Times* publishes secret documents revealing the formation of a special military unit, "to recruit and train suicide squads to carry out terrorist operations in countries opposed to Ayatollah Khomeini's Islamic Republic ... Saudi Arabia, Kuwait, the United Arab Emirates, Jordan and France are named as prime targets of the unit, which is called the 'independent brigade of irregular warfare in enemy territories.'" *The London Times* continues:

"A leading figure behind the creation of the new unit is said to be Mr. Husain Musawi, leader of the Islamic Jihad organization, which has claimed responsibility for suicide attacks in the past three years on American and French establishments in Beirut and Kuwait.

"According to the documents, the support is being requested (by July 1st) of specialized military instructors who should be under 30 years old, preferably bachelors and who 'must be completely committed to martyrdom'... and (July 23rd) some 1,500 to 2,000 men under 30 and preferably bachelors' ... completely committed to martyrdom.'"

The plan also called for "cooperation from the Foreign Ministry to send abroad, in the guise of military attaches ... intelligence agents. Other requests included a secure, isolated base for training the men, and facilities for teaching them to pilot light aircraft and naval vessels." This new unit was deemed necessary because "the increased vigilance of the Arab countries in the region" and the inadequate military training of the terrorist irregulars had "rendered Iran unable to topple the governments opposed to it, except by blows brought to bear from within." The blows brought to bear from within are often carried out by young people, recruited through the mosques or cultural centers, and sent to Iran for "formation."

France, January, 1984. Journalist J.M. Durand-Souffland reports the case of a young Algerian woman, as described by her sister:

"... My parents and I noticed that my sister had changed completely ... She was then sixteen-years-old, in the process of preparing her studies in order to graduate from a Parisian high school. She was a practicing Muslim, but without excessive zeal or ostentation, and regularly frequented a Parisian mosque. There she met Iranian and Lebanese Shi'ites who frequented the center and moved into an apartment provided, rent-free, by the Shi'ites.'The sister adds:

"Two months later ... they were sent to Iran, where they stayed in an 'Islamic school' at Qum.

"In order to learn more, the sister went to enquire at the Paraisan cultural center. This is her account":

'They immediately wanted to know who I was, where I lived, what I was doing, how I lived: A real police enquiry, carried out, however, in a courteous but firm manner. I was obliged to answer all the questions, and I am sure they were the object of further verification.

'A Lebanese Shi'ite, expert in the ways of brainwashing, attempted for hours to extol the virtues of fundamentalism.

'For these men, each Muslim man or woman, old or young, must fight so that divine law might triumph. It is the only way to save oneself from sin, from a corrupt world living in error, injustice and tyranny. All the speeches I listened to concerned the disinherited and the oppressed, whose pitiful condition were caused by the leaders of their respective countries. Little by little, they try to convince the listener of his or her responsibility for this state of affairs, with the help of arguments of this kind: 'What have you done, you who are a Muslim, to change all that? Then it is time to repent, redeem yourself. Come and join us and our fight.'"[128]

Women have their place in this crusade. While they have few civil rights in present day Iran, Khomeini has proclaimed their "right and duty to defend Islam." Zahra Rahnavard Mussavi, the wife of his prime minister, immediately becomes an ardent militant and recruiter. Each mosque (Tehran alone has 3200) must provide eight young women, fully trained for the cause. Military preparation takes place in the numerous camps established since 1979, on the outskirts of all the major towns. On Iranian television, Zahra displays the European and American "sisters" who have joined the cause of Islam. Bernadette Durand, re-baptized "Fatima," declares: "I know how to use arms and explosives. I am ready to sacrifice my life. But before I do, I will destroy dozens of atheists and become a martyr." She is followed by Wendy Santiago, a young woman of South American origin, renamed Mariam: "I am a Kamikaze. I love Allah."

Recruitment of young people is not always accomplished by conventional "brainwashing" methods. A 16 year old Lebanese car bomber, the first to be seized alive by Israeli troops, was questioned at length and interviewed by *The New York Times*. The *Times* article noted:

> "What seems most striking about Mr. Burros account is that although he is a Shi'ite Muslim, he comes from a secular family background. He spent his free time not in prayer, he said, but riding his motorcycle and playing pinball. According to his account, he was not a fanatic who wanted to kill himself in the cause of Islam or anti-Zionism, but was recruited for the suicide mission through another means: Blackmail.
>
> "Shi'ite extremist groups in Lebanon and Iran have given the impression that the suicide bomb attacks have been carried out by devoutly religious people eager to become martyrs..."[129]

The article went on to report that the boy, Mohammed Mahmoud Burro, had been involved in a motorcycle accident. He sought help from Abu Hassan, the Amal security chief in the region, who assured him that the matter was closed. Subsequently his father was involved in an auto accident, resulting in severe financial pressure on the Burro family. Once again the boy sought Amal's help. Now, Abu Hassan responded with "a carefully balanced combination of inducements and threats," telling the boy his family's future was in his hands, offering solutions if he agreed to a suicide mission. These techniques are not new; they have been employed by the Russians, the Chinese, the Cubans, etc. They are the tools of revolutionary professionals—as are the techniques being exported by the mullahs worldwide today.

If there is any lingering doubt that the overthrow of the Shah's government was organized by trained professionals, rather than the result of a "general" uprising, they can be dispelled by reading Montazeri's "Manual of Islamic Revolution."

This manual has been printed in several languages, and advises its readers on how to overthrow an established regime. It offers instruction on how to establish committees to organize the masses; how to steal arms and hide them in mosques, embassies and cultural centers; how to organize street riots; how to incite the forces of law and order to open fire on crowds.

This "bible" of revolution gives instruction on how to create a "psychosis of the blood," which acts as a "powerful drug" on the masses, provoking their anger against the existing regime and generating determination to act against it. Among the recommendations: Cover the feet and garments of demonstrators with mutton blood or Mercurochrome, so it will appear they have been wounded by the forces of order; utilize common burials, accompanied by "wailers" as an occasion for anti-government riots; organize nightly mock street combats, using tapes of machine gun fire, amplified by loudspeakers, to frighten the populace; utilize "unclean" animals like dogs and pigs, and scatter them through the streets, with the names of "hated" leaders attached to their necks; organize public prayers; burn places of sin (bars, cinemas, cabarets, etc.); attack all aspects of the "stinking western civilization"; employ the technique of coffins containing arms, to be used when the police arrive; set fire to old tires, automobiles, etc.; bring in as many press and media representatives as possible; position the mullahs, as well as women and children, in the front ranks, to unsettle the police and make them hesitate to fire their weapons; distribute flowers to the police; feed demonstrators, so they will stay on the streets as long as possible. Recommendations are made for weakening and paralyzing the existing regime: Boycott of western products; nonpayment of utility bills; nonpayment of taxes; organization of traffic bottlenecks; strikes and acts of sabotage.

To anyone who observed the events of the last two years of my brother's reign, Montazeri's manual will have a familiar ring. That these events will repeat themselves elsewhere is promised in the ayatollah's preface:

"In the name of Allah, clement and merciful, if we wish to present in an objective and subjective manner, the content of the Islamic revolution and its line of progress until the final victory, we can say it is the quest for martyrdom in its full meaning that brought to the revolution its victory. The Islamic revolution had its tactics and its techniques of propaganda, of political war, of economic war, of military fighting in its phase of revolutionary destruction. We are going to explain certain facts of the revolution. Here are the techniques that the revolutionaries employed in order to destroy the satanic regime of the Shah ...

"This type of action that we have employed in Iran to overthrow the Shah can become a model for revolution in all Islamic countries throughout the world."

TERRORISM: Beirut, Sunday, October 23, 1983, 6 A.M. A "suicide truck" carrying twelve hundred tons of TNT breaks through the sandbag barricade surrounding the U. S. Marine base. There is a deafening explosion and the facility is instantly reduced to a mass of twisted metal and concrete rubble. Close to 6:30, another explosion is heard, this time in the town, as a second truck destroys the headquarters of the French forces.

The explosions kill 241 Americans, and 58 French. This is the most lethal act of terrorism committed against Westerners in the Lebanese capitol, but not the first:

- In April 1979, the U.S. Embassy and Cultural Center are damaged by mortar shots and grenades;
- In March 1981, the American ambassador escapes an assassination attempt;
- In May 1982, an attack outside the French Embassy leaves many dead and wounded;
- In April 1983, the American Embassy is destroyed by a booby-trapped car loaded with explosives.

And, the attacks continue: In January 1984, the President of the American University of Beirut is assassinated; in June, there is a bomb explosion in the Brish cultural center; also in June, an Austrian diplomat is assassinated; in July, another attack on the American Embassy... Credit for these attacks is claimed by the "Islamic Jihad" or the "Hezbollah." For a time there appears to be some confusion as to who their terrorists are, and whose direction they follow.

April, 1983: Following the attack on the American Embassy, CBS reports that the U.S. secret services had intercepted a series of coded cables, sent by the Iranian Foreign Ministry to the Iranian Embassy in Beirut. One approved the payment of $25,000 for an attack on an unspecified target in Beirut; another instructed the embassy to give assistance to twelve Iranians traveling through Damascus, en route to Beirut, shortly before the U.S. Embassy bombing. Following the mining of the Red Sea, official Iranian radio claims the victory on behalf of the "Islamic Jihad," but once again denies the responsibility of the Iranian government.

Their position is understandable: At this time, Khomeini cannot afford a direct confrontation with the U.S. If he were to be directly implicated in terrorist raids throughout the Middle East, the U.S. could pressure its allies to stop purchasing Iranian oil, the only source of revenue in the Islamic Republic. The embargo on arms he needs in the war with Iraq could become tighter. Far better for him to take the position that the attacks are the work of religious zealots.

December 4, 1984: Terrorists seize a Kuwaiti airliner bound for Pakistan and hijack it to Tehran. They demand the release of 17 convicted terrorists in Kuwaiti jails. Five days later, the hijackers are seized at Tehran airport. Two Americans, employees of the United States Agency for International Development, have been killed, others tortured and abused. In its reports on the incident, *The New York Times* (December 19, 1984) cites a *Reader's Digest* article based on months of interviews with intelligence and anti-terrorist experts, Iranian exiles and unidentified members of the Tehran government. The article states that Iran was using its European embassies as "conduits for weapons and explosives for such terrorist acts as the 1983 attack on the Marine garrison in Beirut." It goes on to say that "In June 1982, an employee of Khomeini's Bern Embassy secretly purchased 300 tons of the lethal explosive cyclonite from a weapons broker in Brussels. Shipped in disguise to Lebanon via India, the explosives are believed to have been used in the suicide attack on the U.S. Marines barracks in Beirut." The article quotes former Iranian Prime Minister Ali Amni, who said that Khomeini's followers in the U.S. had been increasing for the past 15 years, that they "are very well hidden and financed." It went on to say that these groups, under the cover of teaching religious classes in Shilism, have enlisted militant black prison inmates who have converted to Islam. "Upon release, these men joined Khomeini's American terrorist apparatus."

I find it curious that there is the tendency in western circles to accept this position. At the time of the first attempt against the U.S. Embassy (April, 1983) and the raid on the Marine facility (October 1983), the possibility of an "Iranian network" was acknowledged. On October 24, 1983, Secretary of Defense Caspar Weinberger said: "There is a lot of circumstantial evidence that points towards Iran." Later, in an interview with Peter Jennings on ABC, Secretary of State George Schultz said: "There is some circumstantial evidence pointing towards some countries." When Jennings asked if he referred to Iran or Syria, Schultz would not give a direct answer. On September 21, 1984, *The New York Times* said: "The President, at the urging of Secretary of State George P. Schultz, decided on a restrained response, officials said." The official American position appears to be one of readiness to punish those who are "really responsible," but only upon the presentation of "decisive" proof.

This reminds me of a joke that was popular in pre-World War II times, when, it was said, Hitler disguised his spies as tourists. An English policeman approaches a German in Tyrolian attire, in the process of photographing an arsenal. "Are you the spy 009?" asks the bobby. "No," answers the tourist." "I am the spy 005." "Oh," the policeman apologizes, "in that case, I am sorry to have disturbed you." American restraint was understandable when State Department officials were in the process of conducting delicate negotiations for the evacuation of south Lebanon by the Israelis. This was not a time to provoke the Syrians, who cooperate with Khomeini's agents. But after charges of "negligence" are made by Democrats, the administration does reveal that its secret services have proof incriminating the Hezbollah, a Shi'ite organization working with Iran.

January 25, 1984. The results of an in-depth investigation of the Iranian network in Baalbek by journalists Mohamed Selhami and Hamza Kaidi are published in *Jeune Afrigue*. It reveals that the Supreme Council of the Iraqi Islamic Revolution, presided over by Muhammad Bakr al Hakim, with the objective of overthrowing the regime of Saddam Hussein, has another purpose: To function as a cover for terrorist activities. According to *Jeune Afrigue*, the Council has, in Syria, a group described as "coordinators of operations," which includes Khomeini's ambassador to Damascus. Several groups depend on the Council, for funding and assistance: The Mujahiddin (created in Tehran in 1980); Al Amal al Islami (created in Tehran in 1979); and Al Dawa (created in Iraq in 1956). The Council also works closely with a dissident branch of the Lebanese Shi'ite group Amal, headed by Hussein Mussavi, who established his organization in Baalbek under the protection of the Syrian army.

These diverse groups operate "formation" and training camps in Iran (Ahwaz, Tehran and Qum), in Syria (Damascus) and Lebanon (Baalbek). Their activities range from the propagation of the Khomeinist faith to direct military action and terrorism. For certain operations, their commandos take the name of "Islamic Jihad."

According to *Jeune Afrigue*:

"Very quickly Mussavi's men (about 600) become operational. October 23, 1983: Two suicide trucks simultaneously destroy in Beirut the headquarters of the 8th battalion of the U.S. Marines (241 dead) and the command post 'Drakkarl of the first French regiment (58 dead). November 4th: A booby-trapped truck explodes outside the headquarters of the Israeli Army in Tyre. Balance sheet: About 60 slain, including 32 Lebanese and Palestinian prisoners." Mohamed Selhami, who had been authorized to visit the camps, states that each of Mussawi's operations —requires authorization from Damascus. The instructors, he says, include Iranians, Syrians, Libyans, Pakistanis, as well as Europeans and Americans. Recruiting is done in all Islamic countries, in Europe and even in the United States. In this connection, the *London Sunday Times* reported:

"In London, recruitment of the terrorists, called lensan enteharil (suicide men) is led by a slender white turbaned ayatollah, Azhari Qomi, former prosecutor general of revolutionary Iran. He arrived in Britain about five months ago. In October, 4 million pounds deposited in a special account with a British Bank in Jersey was placed at his disposal.

"In Rome, the recruit agent is Ayatollah Hadi Khosrowshahi, whose official title is ambassador to the Vatican. His section of the terror network extends to France and Spain as well as Italy ...

"The suicide-men recruited in London and Rome are from several Muslim countries, including Pakistan, Tunisia and Turkey. They attend special Islamic courses before going to three training camps in Iran."[130]

July 26, 1984. An Agence France Presse dispatch reports that Jafar Niknam, the cultural attache of the Iranian Embassy in Madrid, has been implicated in a terrorist plot involving a Saudi airplane. He is expelled from Spain. The Iranian government denies any knowledge of the case. I investigate this case more closely, for it sheds some light on the nature of Khomeini's operations in the West. I learn that in December 1982, the French police arrested, at Orly Airport, an Iranian who was boarding a plane to Madrid with four kilos of explosives. Sewn to the lining of his jacket was a paper bearing the name "Sayed" and a foreign telephone number. The police alerted Interpol. In January 1983, Spanish authorities learned that the telephone number in question belongs to Sayed Jabar Husseiny, an Iranian who had disappeared from his Madrid apartment.

Eighteen months later, the police located "Sayed" at the Islamic center of Barcelona. At first their surveillance revealed nothing, except Sayed's tendency to spend his evenings with prostitutes and homosexuals. One day, however, Sayed flew to Madrid, spent a few hours at the airport, inspecting the facilities, then proceeded to the apartment of Jafar Niknam, the Iranian cultural attache. After returning to Barcelona, Sayed made a number of trips to Madrid, each time spending several hours at the airport (Police theorized he was monitoring the arrival times of Saudi and Kuwait airliners). On July 20, another Iranian, carrying a false Tunisian passport, arrived in Madrid and met with Jafar Niknam.

The police uncovered details of the plot: The bogus Tunisian was an assassin, assigned to murder members of the Iranian opposition in exile. He was to proceed to the airport, wait for two "associates" from Tehran, then fly to Saudi Arabia. Under cover of their diplomatic passports, Sayed and Niknam were to carry the assassin's weapons through customs, then return them to him in the waiting area. On July 23rd, the police made their arrests, uncovering an arsenal of weapons in the Islamic center in Barcelona.

Terrorism is an important political tool for Khomeini, who has thus far been unable to successfully export his Islamic Republic to other countries. The president of his parliament, Rafsanjani, has this to say to the official newspaper *Joumhouriye Eslami*:

"That an American soldier is killed in Lebanon profits us more than the liquidation of 200 Phalangists (Christian militia). That the Lebanese people kill a French soldier with a bullet profits us more than the exploding of a hydrogen bomb by one or another so-called Islamic countries."[131]

The editorialist of the propaganda organ of Amal al Islami adds:

"The intelligence services which made us tremble with fear are today, thanks to our courage, obsessed with dynamite. Each day, they await a new explosion, here or there, which will destroy their cardboard bunkers in Beirut, Baghdad, Kuwait, and even in Washington and Paris, or other capitols which have become a staging area for our martyrs."[132]

Khomeini did not invent political terror. Though his followers have made their own innovations, they are part of an international problem, described quite well by Claire Sterling in her book *Terror Network*.[133] As I read this book, I recalled the "Tri-continental Congress" held in Havana in January 1966, which I have mentioned before. At the time, our intelligence services had noted the participation of several Iranians describing themselves as students, among them Sadegh Ghotbzadeh. The Congress recommended close cooperation between the "socialist countries" and "national liberation movements." It devised a revolutionary strategy, which included guerrilla warfare and terrorism, against "U.S. imperialism." It called for coordination with "student and workers' movements" in western countries, as well as in the Third World. At the time, the Cubans had their own training camps. Moscow dispatched Colonel Vadim Kotchergin to Cuba, to create new camps, and soon the Palestinians and Europeans were invited to participate. By 1970 the Palestinians had created camps in Syria and North

Lebanon, to be followed later by camps in Libya. In South Yemen, the Soviets established a kind of "university" of terrorism and guerrilla warfare. According to Claire Sterling, the "students" in the camps around Aden included members of West Germany's Baader-Meinhof group, Italy's Red Brigades, the Basque ETA, the Provisional IRA, the Japanese Red Army, the Tupamaros of Uruguay and the Turkish and Iranian underground. Sterling adds:

"There is massive proof that the Soviet Union and its surrogates, over the last decade, have provided the weapons, training and sanctuary for a worldwide terror network aimed at the destabilization of western democratic society.

"The network, as described by dozens of captured terrorists and volumes of courtroom testimony, consists of a multitude of disparate groups, helping one another and receiving indispensable aid from not altogether disinterested outsiders."[134]

I have already noted that the student movements of 1968, in France and the U.S., were the first manifestations of the Havana Congress. I don't know the intelligence services of the West reported this Congress, but ours in Iran minimized its potential. They convinced my brother that it was merely a reaction to the "consumer societies" of the West, which the communists were attempting to exploit. They said it would suffice to keep leftist agents in Iran under surveillance.

Paris, August 23, 1973. George Pompidou, President of the Republic of France, receives a confidential memo entitled "Palestine-Libya, Fedayan activities in Europe" from his secret services. The memo revealed that the Libyan ambassador was housing a group of 30 Palestinian terrorists belonging to the FPLP (Popular Front for the Liberation of Palestine), recently arrived from Beirut and Tripoli. The Italian secret services were informed of the imminent beginning of a massive terrorist operation in Europe, financed by Libya.[135] The first attack took place on December 17, 1973, at Fiumicino Airport. Engineer Corado of ENI (the Italian State Oil organization) boarded a Pan American flight to Iran. Shortly before takeoff, an explosion destroyed the aircraft, leaving 35 burned bodies, including that of Carat.

Italy found herself in the midst of an international crime wave financed by Qaddafi's oil revenues. Investigation showed that the transfer of funds was carried out by Libyan embassies, through numbered accounts in Swiss banks. Members of the secret services of Tripoli (including terrorists of various nationalities) were attached to Libyan embassies, or traveled with Lebanese, Moroccan, Tunisian, Syrian or Iranian passports. The infrastructure of this terror network has a diplomatic base (individual embassies being more or less important, depending on the tolerance of the host country). In addition, Qaddafi stationed paid assassins (Palestinians, Japanese, Italian, French, etc.) in various capitols and recruited terrorist trainees from the ranks of extremist students. Libyan agents developed a network of sympathizers among student and revolutionary organizations which had no distinct political orientation.

In 1974, the European center of operations was transferred to the Federal Republic of Germany. The armaments section was installed in Zurich.[136] In 1981, it was discovered that five years before, a former CIA agent had contracted with Qaddafi to furnish the Libyan dictator with explosives and to teach his agents the latest terrorist techniques. Former CIA agent Edwin P. Wilson had, with Frank E. Terpil, another former agent, created a commercial company for the purchase, export and transfer of materials needed by the Libyans. This operation continued until Wilson's arrest and trial, following the discovery of documents in the company's secret files, documents which outlined "a training program for intelligence and security officers in the field of espionage, sabotage and general psychological warfare ... with an emphasis on the design, manufacture, implementation and detonation of explosive devices."[137]

Ever increasing terrorist activities throughout the world have led authorities to consider the possibility of an international network. Acts of cooperation between diverse groups reinforces this hypothesis. The attack on Israeli athletes at the 1972 Olympics, followed by the massacre at Lod airport by the Japanese Red Army, the smuggling of sabotage material into Israel by a German couple, the attack on Trieste oil installations by Algerian terrorists—these incidents brought to light such cooperation.

It is known that there were ties between Palestinian organizations and terrorist groups in Argentina, Uruguay, Peru, Venezuela, Turkey and Iran. As early as 1970, George Habash, head of the FPFP, accepted Japanese and Iranians in his training camps, yet the question of an international network was not reactivated in the West until 1982, when American Lieutenant Colonel Ray was assassinated in Paris and General Dozier was kidnaped in Italy. An editorial in *Le Monde* notes:

"The bloody operation was to be launched against the Christian democracy (Italy) on the occasion of its next national council had in appearance an exclusively Italian character. But the nature of the armaments which were to be used, and the more and more frequent declarations of political leaders of all persuasions, and recently, the words of Judge Imposimato, lead to talk again on the ties between the underworld, certain secret services thirsty for the destabilization of democracies and various terrorist movements.

"In fact the existence of such ties are not new and particular to Italy. That the Japanese Red Army, for example trains with the Palestinians and utilizes their arsenals, there is no doubt. It has also been established that elements of Italy's extreme left went to the Middle East on several occasions to find arms. And it is in Beirut that credit for the assassination of the American diplomat in Paris was taken.

"Do these obvious contacts ... enable us to speak of a truly international plot? The answer to this question depends no doubt on the degree of coordination beyond which it can be designated a concerted offensive. The coincidence of certain dates (for example, the great turn of Italian terrorism in 1974-75 and the beginning of Armenian terrorism) obliges us to raise the question, though we may feel some skepticism regarding the thesis, once defended by the French Interior Minister, of a 'clandestine orchestra leader'..."[138]

Judge Imposimato, to whom the editorial refers, headed the second inquiry into the Moro affair. In January 1982, he affirmed that there existed an international plot to destabilize Italy, with ties to Libyan organizations, the Israeli secret services, and the KGB.

A key figure in the international network is Libya's Qaddafi, who has served as mentor and aide to Khomeini. Today we can see a startling similarity in their speeches and their methods. In February 1983, for example, Qaddafi invited delegates to the "Congress of Arab People" to violently confront the authorities of their countries. On May 1, 1984, Workers' Day, he called for the workers of the world to "abolish salaries and liberate themselves from servitude to their employers: Governments, individuals, private and public companies." He added: "Workers must refuse to listen to speeches which do not invite them to free themselves from salaries and servitude to the employer ... The first of May has become the day of global cheating against the salaried of the earth."[139] With his enormous oil revenues, the Libyan dictator funds and supports diverse terrorist groups. Each year, for example, he provides the PLO with $75 million; in 1976, he remitted $16 million to George Habash's FPLP, for the assassination of Egypt's President Sadat. On occasion he has resorted to direct military intervention, as he did in Chad. After Khomeini's students seized the American Embassy, Qaddafi had this to say, in an interview with Oriana Fallaci:

"When an embassy or some members of an embassy commit acts that go beyond their functions, that are damaging to the host country, reactions such as those in Tehran may follow. Embassies cannot be granted diplomatic immunity when they perform the kind of acts I said.

"I am very happy that the Iranian revolution has happened and that it has been successful twice: First in kicking out the Shah and second in kicking out the

Americans. I would even go so far as to say that my revolutionary role has been strengthened by the Iranian revolution. And I want to repeat that in case of an American attack against Iran, even apart from this episode, we will not remain with our hands tied."[140]

There is an interesting ambiguity in America's relations with Qaddafi. Despite his anti-American activities, the U.S. has intervened on a number of actions to protect him from his opposition. On at least one occasion, Qaddafi was warned by CIA agents in Libya of political conspiracies directed against him. On several occasions, the CIA, working with British and Italian services, thwarted plots to assassinate the Libyan dictator.[141] In 1983, a former U.S. intelligence analyst revealed that the U.S. Embassy in Tripoli had foiled a planned military coup to overthrow Qaddafi in 1971. Asked what motive the U.S. might have had for thwarting the coup, the analyst replied: "Oil is a very big interest. There are economic oil interests in Libya that did not want to see the change."[141] I have seen a similar ambiguity in the U.S. attitude toward Khomeini. And I suspect it may be true that it was the British and Americans who warned the ayatollah in 1979 of a conspiracy, and who supplied the information which led to the arrest and execution of some fifty civilians and military men. Relations between Qaddafi and Khomeini were briefly clouded in the Fall of 1978, when Musa Sadr, the Iranian Imam of the Lebanese Shi'ites in Lebanon disappeared in Libya (he was, in fact, assassinated, on Qaddafi's orders). However after Khomeini returned to Tehran, he was secretly reconciled with Qaddafi, through the mediation of Syria's President Assad.

Once in power, Khomeini put into practice all the terrorist techniques learned and borrowed from his Libyan (and Palestinian) allies. Secret documents and cables spirited from Khomeini's embassies by the opposition show that the ayatollah has surpassed Qaddafi in his use of embassies and cultural institutions as cover for terrorist activity. Like Qaddafi, he employs hired killers (trained by the Palestinians and Libyans) to dispose of political opponents in exile (in 1981, Ali Tabatabai, president of the Iranian Freedom Foundation; in 1984, former General Oveissi, along with his brother.) There is more to Khomeini's Jihad than random acts of violence. Islamic societies must be infiltrated, their leaders undermined and replaced; western societies subverted and divided. His ideology is more effective than that of his Libyan colleague, for it derives legitimacy from the Koran and from his personal role as interpreter of Allah's Will. Until 1979, Qaddafi was the principal support and inspiration for Muslim extremists. Today it is to Tehran that these groups look, for Khomeini has made of terrorism an instrument of his holy war. In the pursuit of his goals, he has even managed to procure American arms:

"From excellent sources we have learned that Colonel Azizi, responsible for the procurement of official arms for Iran has achieved a master stroke in the purchase, from the United States, several stocks of air to air and air to sea missiles. In principle, these arms under embargo cannot be sent to Iran. But Azizi never directly appeared on the scene or in the transactions. It is a European firm which closed this amazing deal in the U.S. with official documents. Officially, the missiles were destined for an Arab country allied with the United States. Other buyers, from South American, purchased arms in the names of their countries, while in fact all these arms were secretly shipped to Iran."[142]

To coordinate and supervise terrorist and revolutionary activities Khomeini has created specific organizations which operate from Tehran. In September 1981, the "Council of Islamic Revolution" was created to supervise all subversive activities, particularly those in the Islamic world. The president of this council is the Hojatoleslam Mohammad Taghi Mudaresi, who also directs the "Party for Islamic Action," whose goal is the overthrow of the governments of Bahrain and the Gulf Emirates. Vice president is Hojatoleslam Muhammad Bagher Hakim of Iraq. The members are: Hojatoleslam Hadi Mudaresi, former

Khomeini representative to Bahrain; Kuwaiti Mehdi Musavi;
Hojatoleslam Ali Akbar Mohtashemi, Iran's ambassador to Damascus; the Lebanese mullah Jalaledin Saghir; the Iraqi Ahmad
Al-Heydari; Abbas Mehri, Khomeini's cousin and former representative in Kuwait; the Lebanese Saeed Al-Hosseini; Ahmad
Nekhavalei, a Shi'ite leader in Saudi Arabia; the Kurd Mehdi
Zarivand. The Council functions as a financing, planning and
coordinating organ. A representative of the Pasdarans is present
at all meetings. The Council is made up of five sections:

- The Supreme Council of the Islamic Revolution of Iraq,
  presided over by Hojatoleslam Muhammad Bagher Hakim,
  includes the Iraqi Shi'ite Party Al-Daawa, as well as Iraqi and
  Kurdish Mujahedeen. The Hojatoleslam Muhammad Mehdi
  Hakim (who generally resides in the UK) is responsible for
  the group's international relations, while the Hojatoleslam
  Bahr-al-oloum directs secret operations.

- The Supreme Council of the Islamic Revolution of Syria and
  Lebanon, presided over by the Lebanese Shi'ite Sheikh
  Jaafari, includes dissident Amal-ist Hussein Mussavi and
  Sheikh Yaghi, chief of the Lebanese Hazbollah. Mussavi's
  militia (which includes the suicide-men) carries out opera-
  tions for the council.

- The Supreme Council of the Islamic Revolution of the Arabian Peninsula is directed by Hojatoleslam Muhammad
  Taghi Mudaressi (who has already engineered several un-
  successful subversive operations in Bahrain, Saudi Arabia
  and Kuwait).

- The Supreme Council of the Islamic Revolution of Africa
  and the Maghreb, under the presidency of Tunsian cleric
  Umar alMasri, includes Moroccan and Egyptian representatives, as well as Khomeini's representative to Libya. This
  council encompasses extremist movements in Nigeria,
  Mauritania and North Africa. (After discovering a terrorist
  network created by this council Senegal severed relations
  with Tehran in 1983.) According to some sources, this

council participated in the plot to assassinate Anwar Sadat, as well as in the disorders in Morocco and Tunisia.

• The Supreme Council of the Islamic Revolution of Asian countries is active also in Turkey and the Muslim Republics of the Soviet Union.

These are the key organs of the Council of Islamic Revolution. They have at their disposal several training camps, for the "formation" of fighting forces and candidates for suicide missions.

Khomeini recognizes the ongoing need for dramatic acts of terror, such as suicide-trucks and the mining of the Red Sea, in order to sustain the fervor of his youthful activists. Therefore he has set up a special group for this purpose in cooperation with the Pasdarans, and directed by Mehdi Hashemi. Its budget includes government subsidies, contributions from Bazaar merchants, exiled Iraqi Shi'ites and Iranians residing abroad.

The terrorist movement launched by Khomeini in Arab and western countries will survive his regime. In a sense it is more dangerous than Khomeini himself, for the movement includes many diverse elements with local motivations. As long as it remains unidentified, allowed to operate with impunity, it will grow stronger and bolder with each success—and increasingly difficult to stop.

April 1984. At a meeting of the "Tri-Lateral Commission" (a group of prominent citizens of North America, western Europe and Japan), American Secretary of State George Schultz speaks:

"How do we combat this challenge? Certainly we must take security precautions to protect our people and our facilities. Certainly we must strengthen our intelligence capabilities to alert ourselves to the threats.

"But it is increasingly doubtful that a purely passive strategy can even begin to cope with the problem. This raises a host of questions for a free society: In what circumstance and how should we respond? When and how should we take preventive or preemptive action against known terrorist groups? What evidence do we insist upon before taking such steps?

"As the threats mount and as the involvement of such countries as Iran, Syria, Libya and North Korea has become more and more evident, then it is more appropriate that the nations of the West face up to the need for active defense against terrorism ... Once it is established that terrorism works—that it achieves its political objectives—its practitioners will become bolder and the threat to us will be all the greater."

10: CONCLUSION—
MY UNTOLD STORY

I STILL HAVE TEARS TO CRY: I am neither an academic nor a political analyst, but I have spent most of my life on the political scene. And in the years of exile, I have never stopped collecting information about the upheaval that shook my country, ended the Pahlavi monarchy and made Iran "a country that never smiles." In the books, newspapers, documents and journals which fill my library, in long conversations with other Iranian exiles, I hoped to find fuller answers to questions of "how" and "why", to clarify a picture that was sketchy and rather confused six years ago. I am not, nor do I claim to be, the most objective observer of these events. But I believe mine is a legitimate point of view, one which could not be heard in the highly emotional climate following the "Islamic Revolution" and during the hostage crisis.

I chose to make public my notes and observations now because time has passed, more facts have come to light—enough to allow a reevaluation of my brother's reign *within a regional framework*, an examination of the forces which led to his overthrow, and a clear look at the nature of the regime which replaced him. In the light of information now at hand—disclosures made in books and articles, secret documents uncovered, the personal revelations of politicians and diplomats—I think the case can be made for a "conspiracy" theory, if not by design, then certainly by circumstance.

It seems clear that there were three groups working to weaken the ties between the U.S. and the Shah's government: The KGB and its international network; the right wing opposition (former large landowners and Khomeini's followers) in Iran and abroad, which closed ranks with the leftists, to form a solid alliance by the late 1970's; liberal and anti-Shah elements in the Carter administration (reinforced by similar elements in France and England) who favored a "moderate" government made up of the remnants of Mossadegh's National Front Party and the pro-religious "liberals" headed by Mehdi Bazargan.

Yes, the Shah made enemies, as does any Middle Eastern leader, but the West failed to see the opposition as special interest groups, and not as representatives of a "popular" revolutionary force. In a very real sense, this Islamic revolution was not a "popular" revolution at all, but rather a counter-revolution, carried out by those who had been deprived of power and influence by the governments of my father and brother. They support they gathered came about in true Middle Eastern fashion, when signals from abroad and from within communicated that the Shah's regime was doomed.

The West failed to understand this, as they fail so often to understand the fluid and shifting nature of political ideologies and loyalties in the Middle East, the power of the cult of personality. I think the West also failed to understand how its attempt to avoid mistakes made in Latin America, by "hedging" its commitment to an old and steadfast ally, by offering support and encouragement to factions professing "liberal" values, by pressuring my brother to make disastrous and ill-timed accommodations, virtually ensured the disintegration of his government. As a case in point of the pragmatic shifts of Eastern political factions, of the West's consistent misreading of these groups, its readiness to embrace those who pay lip service to popular western values, I offer excerpts from a recent column by Jack Anderson and Joseph Spear in the *Washington Post*:

"About 200 members of Congress have been succored into writing letters of endorsement for a terrorist group whose cadres participated in the 1979 seizure of the U.S. Embassy and American hostages in Iran. In fact, the group advocated putting the hostages on trial as spies, and staged a demonstration protesting their release.

"This militant Marxist organization has sent fast talking Iranian exiles, soaped and pressed and wearing tailored suits and neatly knotted ties, to visit Capitol Hill. They have persuaded gullible lawmakers that they are 'freedom fighters' against Ayatollah Ruhollah Khomeini.

"It's technically true that these Marxist revolutionaries, once pro-Khomeini, turned against him after he began a remorseless crackdown on communist elements in Iran.

"They now call themselves the 'People Mojahedin organization of Iran'—a name that apparently sounds enough like the anti-Soviet Mujahedeen guerrillas in Afghanistan to confuse the unwary.

"We unmasked the Mojahedin terrorists last August and told how they had hoodwinked several members of Congress into writing letters of support.

"Some of the gulled lawmakers quickly repudiated the Mojahedin, but the Iranian Marxists merely redoubled their lobbying efforts on Capitol Hill. Now the State Department has privately warned members of Congress that they are being courted by militants who are devout Marxists, stridently anti-American and violent.

"The department's warning is contained in a one-page summary of an intelligence report on the Iranian exile group. Our associate Lucette Lagnado has obtained the report, which says the group was formed to combat

'U.S. imperialism' and 'criminal Zionism.' These are re-garded by the Mojahedin as 'the principal forces which have corrupted Iran and oppressed the world.'

"According to the document, members of the group 'have advocated the use of violence since their inception' and have participated in 'bombings, assassinations of Iranians, attacks on Israeli offices in Tehran and bank robberies.'"

Understandably, the State Department is wary of those who profess to represent the cause of "freedom" in Iran. If its coun-terparts in the Carter administration had investigated more closely those who claimed to represent the cause of "human rights," I doubt that we would have a terrorist regime in con-trol of Iran today. For the moment the principal beneficiary of this regime is the Soviet Union. The revolution and the war with Iraq have eliminated the dangers posed by a strong Iranian army, equipped and advised by the U.S., on its southern borders. To a lesser extent, the Israelis have benefitted from the military losses suffered by Iraq, though they are now confronted, thanks to Khomeini's intervention, by a stronger Palestinian presence throughout the Middle East.

The truth is that the U.S. has lost a reliable ally, and the people of my country have lost most of all. Those who persist in seeing Khomeini's brand of Islam as a positive force are out of touch with what is happening in Iran today. One of the in-vited guests to Montazeri's conference of Shi'ite Imams, held in Tehran in 1984, was Allameh Mahdi al-Alawi, a Lebanese Shi'ite dignitary whose family was originally from Iran. Appalled by the destruction committed in the name of religion, he spoke out in an interview with the Lebanese magazine *Al Kenar* (published in Cyprus):

"In 1972, I visited the Iran that my father and the Imam Sadr had so often told me about ... When I arrived in Tehran, I was struck by the grandeur and development of the city. At the same time, the westernization that I observed in certain areas and in the conduct of the people disturbed me. For several months I stayed in Qum, where things were quite different. I had philosophy lessons with my great-uncle, Allameh Tabatabai and, in the afternoon, with the Ayatollah Shariat-Madari, a liberal cleric who wanted to cleanse Shilism of superstitions and reactionary ideas, as did our late lamented Imam Sadr.

"I felt a great pride when I saw how Iranians revered the eighth Imam of the Shi'ites and cared for his tomb at Mashad. It is interesting to note that the Shahs, and particularly the late Shah, always made the effort to maintain and improve the site of the Mausoleum of the Imam Reza. I must tell you how astonished I was during my recent visit, when I saw that the new regime had taken all the gold and silver decorations that had adorned it and erased all the inscriptions which showed the efforts of the Shahs to restore the mausoleum."

When the interviewer asked him if he had seen signs of the future revolution, Mahdi al-Alawi answered:

"Not at all. The furthest thing from anyone's mind was revolution. There was discontent, but it had nothing to do with religion. The government respected the demands of religion, and religious leaders enjoyed great respect. During my recent visit, it pained me to see that the people had come to despise and hate men of the cloth...

"How I regret this last trip ... From the moment I disembarked at Tehran airport, I found myself in a city in mourning. There was no longer any trace of the faces full of hope I had seen in 1972. Their situation is even worse than ours in Beirut, in its most tragic moments. We were driven to the best hotel in the city. From my window I could see the sinister Evin Prison, where more than 30,000 prisoners waste away, most them good Muslims at odds with the present regime.

"For the congress they had assembled a group of so called religious leaders from the four corners of the world. I saw that three or four of them never prayed at all. Those participating had been given large sums of money, for the purpose of making payments to members of the government.

"Thanks to my knowledge of Farsi, I was able to talk to some of the Iranian religious leaders under house arrest in Qum, because of their opposition to the regime. They shed tears ... as they told me about the crimes of the regime. In Qum the Ayatollah Rouhani is under surveillance, and the Ayatollah Shariat-Madary, the highest authority on Shi'ism today, is confined to his house, without the right to receive anyone. One of my cousins was in prison, another defrocked by order of the authorities.

"The city of Qum has lost its serenity, under the shadow of machine guns. The natives of Qum refuse to speak to the clerics. The partisans of the regime go around in bulletproof vests, accompanied by bodyguards. And the majority (of the people) who have nothing to do with the regime are in an appalling, lamentable state. One of the professors of the religious school in Qum said to me: 'A thousand times a day I pray to Allah to call me to him, because even my family does not run out of insults for those who wear the turban.'

"In Mashad the situation was worse. My maternal uncle, the Ayatollah Hassan Tabatabai Ghomi, was imprisoned in this house ... The site of the tomb of the eighth Imam was deserted. It was as if ... the Iranian people were turning away from religion because of the acts of the regime."

Asked about the consequences of the war, Mahdi al-Alawi answered:

"Perhaps the best example would be to tell you about the visit that they organized for us, to the central cemetery, called Beheshte-Zahra, of the Capitol. The size of the cemetery had quintupled during the five years of the regime. Tens of thousands of soldiers are buried there, alongside victims of the regime. In one corner of the cemetery, a sort of monument to death has been constructed: a large basin with a jet in the center, which spouts water colored red, to symbolize blood. Imagine that in a great country such a monument can only represent the nature of the regime and the thoughts of the leaders."[143]

Sunni Ulemas have condemned Khomeini's brand of Islam, as have many of the great Shi'ite ayatollahs. In August 1984, the Ayatollah Gopayagani addressed a message to Khomeini, warning him of a "general defection" of the people from Islam.[144] This "defection" by those not directly associated with the regime is described by Mehdi Bazargan, Khomeini's former prime minister:

"Complaints and curses are heard on all sides, everywhere—in the houses, in the streets, in taxis—you hear the people criticize and curse ... Many men and women, young and old, who believed, who revered and worshiped God and followed the teachings of the Koran, of the Prophet and of the Imams, today, in the face of the excesses of Islamic justice, the conduct of the government's agents, and the imposition of its ideas, are now abandoning religion and even Allah. They no longer pray ... They say that everything they had read in books or heard in sermons, about truth, justice and compassion was just a tissue of lies. The true Islam, they add, is what we see around us. Muhammad (the Prophet) and Ali (the first Imam) were just like the mullahs who oppress us."[145]

Even within the repressive climate of Khomeini's regime, the number of demonstrations has increased. In February 1983, the "disinherited" from the south of the capitol (those who

fervently welcomed Khomeini in 1979) took to the streets, protesting the lack of water and electricity, shouting "We want the
Shah." In the parliamentary elections of April 1984, the ballot
boxes yielded thousands of write-in ballots bearing the names
of my brother and his prime minister, Amir Abbas Hoveyda. In
September 1984, 40,000 youths, protesting the regime's policies,
rampaged through the Amjadieh Stadium, chanting "Death to
Khomeini." Khomeini's response is to call out his Revolutionary Guards. His response to the material dissatisfaction of the
Iranian people is this:

"If the Iranians get what they want, they will stop fighting
for the victory of Islam around the world. We must create repeated crises and exalt the idea of death and martyrdom ... It
is in the ardor of these crises that those who are called upon to
export the revolution will lose their unhealthy desire for comfort."[146]

Although the mullahs attempt to project the image of a
stable, if repressive, regime, the situation in Iran is far different
now than what most western reports would have us believe.
Every day, reports from Iran speak of a growing disenchantment
and discontent. The opposition to Khomeini is widespread and
varied. It is not, as was the case during my brother's reign, a
very vocal or well-organized opposition. Many Iranians in exile
have relatives in Iran and fear reprisals. Some have hopes of
recovering their houses and their businesses. Others keep a low
profile so as not to attract the attention of Khomeini's assassins.
All have noticed the tendency of the western media to minimize
the weight and importance of the opposition, to persist in por-
traying the Khomeini regime as "stable," to search hopefully for
signs that a "normalization" of relations may be possible. They
believe, as I sometimes do, that the West would like nothing
more than to sweep this "mistake" under the rug and ignore its
appalling consequences.

Today many educated and sophisticated Iranians believe
that Khomeini's unexpected and rather unbelievable accession
to power was the outcome of an American plan to replace a

progressive and westernized ruler with a backward Islamic theocrat in an attempt to create the first link in a chain of fanatically religious governments around atheist Russia. They maintain that this plan included Islamic governments for Pakistan, Turkey and Afghanistan. In the West, this kind of thinking has been dismissed as "Iranian paranoia." Yet educated Iranians have long been aware of the popularity of the "Islamic Map" theory among western political analysts. (The article I have previously noted, where former Ambassador Sullivan presents his version of this theory, for example, leads me to suspect he held these opinions while he represented the U.S. in Tehran.)

At some point in the late 1960's, Marxists conceived of the idea of subverting Islam, rather than opposing it. Yet my late brother's warnings regarding the dangers of the alliance between Red and Black were ignored. Under the guise of Islam, Khomeini's mullahs have implemented a series of radical measures which no communist regime could have accomplished so readily. An important example is the manner in which Khomeini has dealt with such genuinely representative and popular religious leaders as Shariat Madari, whose opposition to communism is well-known. A leftist regime would have still encountered resistance had it tried to discredit or neutralized him. But Khomeini managed to accomplish this in the name of Islam. He has also generated such as revulsion against religion among the "silent majority" of Iranians that he has effectively neutralized the power of Islam as a barrier to communism. In fact, some Iranians today liken Khomeini to the Trojan horse, saying that he is the vehicle by which communism can be smuggled into Iran.

The "Islamic experiment" in Iran is failing. Despite its constant appeal to religious sentiments and despite the daily executions and repression, the regime is today less secure than ever. Sources in Iran point to the fact that popular opposition has already effectively denied the Khomeini government the degree of stability and recognition it needs to sink its roots. Its militant radicalism leaves no room for modification or "humanization." Its government by terror has alienated the people it rules. The mullahs have managed to retain power by mutilating the civil service and the army (the army, which opposition groups see as the strongest hope for overthrowing the regime, has been kept in line by the growing number of "Pasdarans"), by creating secondary problems (such as the war with Iraq) to divert attention from the serious internal problems, and by creating new vested interest groups whose survival is tied to the Islamic regime.

There is a strong and growing opposition in the country which tries, at great risk, to communicate these views to the outside world. This opposition is disheartened by what it sees as a lack of interest on the part of the west in the suffering of the Iranian people. They look to Iranian exiles in the West to publicize their plight. I count myself among their number, and I recognize that our efforts are handicapped by a number of factors. We oppose a regime which ostensibly came into power on a wave of popular support, gathered from a widespread resentment against a monarch who was pictured as corrupt and repressive. Indeed, western public opinion was so anti-Shah, and by extension, in favor of his adversary, that opposition groups now must fight on two fronts: to counter Khomeini's propaganda offensive on one side, and to challenge western thinking that the situation in Iran before the revolution was as hopeless as it is now. This constant preoccupation with how to explain the prerevolutionary era has been a divisive factor among exile groups.

The Islamic regime has exploited the divisions within opposition ranks, saying none of them is capable of providing a viable alternative. At home, the mullahs suppress dissident voices, and to the West they present the following arguments:

1. Their regime has a vast popular base, and if it appears backward, repressive and different from other regional governments, that is because the people wish it to be so;

2. The overriding concern of the people is neither material comfort nor political freedom, but a fanatical devotion to

religious formalism (with those Iranians who would prefer a more progressive system being a tiny minority);

3. The only alternatives to the theocracy are the disintegration of Iran or a leftist, possibly communist government.

The opposition groups fear that the West may accept these arguments and subsequently try to reach an accommodation with the mullahs, in the hope that time and western influence will "soften" and "liberalize" the theocracy. If that happens, Iran may well sink deeper into the dark ages, to the point where the efforts of the centrist opposition will prove futile, and to the point where the only hope of rescue may be provided by the communists.

Today, many Iranians feel that the protest movement in 1978 which subsequently developed into the revolution has been thoroughly misrepresented by the mullahs, the leftists, the intelligentsia and the international media. They said they never envisioned the creation of a theocracy. The powerful bazaaris and some nationalist politicians now say they were guilty of political naivete in supporting the mullahs or in failing to offer resistance. They feel they have paid a heavy price for those mistakes, and they look to the West to recognize the nature of its miscalculations.

For my part, I refuse to give way to pessimism. I cannot and will not believe that six decades of progress can be so easily obliterated. I know that many western politicians and business interests favor normalization of relations with Khomeini's Iran. Yet I hope that common sense (if not a sense of social conscience) and the lessons of history, will prevail, will raise the question of "what price accommodation?" with a government that violates the most basic of human rights and bases itself on concepts that strikingly suggest Hitler's Germany. I hope that the West can put aside short-term goals in favor of a well-reasoned long-term policy. For if the centrist opposition to Khomeini is left unsupported, the people of Iran may well see communism as the only hope of deliverance from the mullahs.

But there *is* a viable alternative to the Black and the Red, and it lies in an Iranian nation under a constitutional monarchy which can assure the peaceful coexistence of all religious beliefs and ethnic diversity. It is up to Iranians to put aside differences which only profit the extreme Left and the extreme Right, to fight together for a unified Iran, to rebuild, for their children, the heritage of a strong and vital country.

EPILOGUE

Of the many newspaper clippings I have kept throughout these painful years of exile, there is one which always comes to mind. It has turned yellow with the passage of time, but up to this day of March, 1995, it has retained all of its actuality. It was written by Roger Scruton and printed in the London Times of November 6, 1994 under the title "Danger Wreckers Still At Work." I would like to share it with the reader for indeed it addresses a number of ethical questions.

"**Who remembers** Iran? **Who remembers**, that is, the shameful stampede of western journalists and intellectuals to the cause of the Iranian revolution? **Who remembers** the hysterical propaganda campaign waged against the Shah, the—press reports of corruption, police oppression, palace decadence, constitutional crisis? **Who remembers** the thousands of Iranian students in western universities, enthusiastically absorbing the fashionable Marxist nonsense purveyed to them be armchair radicals, so as one day to lead the campaign of riot and mendacity which preceded the Shah's downfall?

Who remembers the behavior of those students who held as hostage the envoys of the very same power which had provided them their "educations"? Who remembers Edward Kennedy's accusation, that the Shah had presided over "one of the most oppressive regimes in history," and had stolen "umpteen billions of dollars from Iran"?

And **who remembers**, the occasional truth that our journalists enabled us to glimpse, concerning the Shah's real achievements, his successes in combating illiteracy, back wardress and powerlessness of his country, his enlightened economic policy, the reforms which might have saved his people from the tyranny of evil mullahs, had he been given the chance to accomplish them? **Who remembers** the freedom and security in which journalists could roam Iran gathering the gossip that would fuel their fanciful stories of a reign of terror?

True the Shah was an autocrat. But autocracy and tyranny are not the same. An autocrat may preside, as the Shah sought to preside, over a representative parliament over and independent judiciary, even over a free press and autonomous universities.

The Shah like Kemal Ataturk, whose, vision he shared regarded his autocracy as the means to the creation and protection of such institutions. **Why** did no one among the western political scientists trouble to point this out, or to rehearse the theory which tells us to esteem not just the democratic process, but also the representative and limiting institutions which may still flourish in its absence? **Why** did no one enjoin us to compare the political system of Iran with that or Iraq or Syria? **Why** did our political scientists rush to embrace the Iranian revolution, despite the evidence that revolution in these circumstances must be the prelude to massive social disorder and a regime of terror?

Why did the western intelligence go on repeating the myth that the Shah was to blame for this revolution, when both Khomeini and the Marxists had been planning it for thirty years, and had found, despite their many attempts to put it into operation only spasmodic popular support?

The answer to all these questions is simple. The Shah was an ally of the West, whose achievement in establishing limited monarchy in a vital strategic region had helped to guarantee our security, to bring stability to the Middle East, and to defer Soviet expansion. The Shah made the fatal mistake of supposing that the makers of western opinion would love him for creating conditions which guaranteed their freedom. On the contrary, they hated him. The Shah had reckoned without the great death wish that haunts our civilization and which causes vociferous members to propagate any falsehood, however absurd provided only that it damages our chances of survival.

For a while of course, those vociferous elements will remain silent on the embarrassing topic of the collapse of Iranian institutions, the establishment of religious terror and the end of stability in the region. **Those who lent their support to this tragedy simply turned their back on it and went elsewhere,** to prepare a similar outcome for the people of Turkey, Egypt, Algeria, El Salvador—or wherever else our vital interests may be damaged.

Of course, it is difficult now for a western correspondent to enter Iran, and if he did so it would not be fun. He would have to witness quietly, and in terror of his life, things which beggar description—the spontaneous "justice" of revolutionary guards the appalling scenes of violence, torture and demonic frenzy, the public humiliation of women, daily sacrifices of lives too young to be conscious of the meaning for which they are condemned to destruction.

He would also have to confront the truth which has been staring in the face for years, and which he could still recognize had the habit of confessing to his errors been preserved; the truth that limited monarchy is the **right** form of government for Iran which can be saved only by the restoration of the Shah's legitimate successor. But such a result would be in the interests, not only of the Iranian people, but also of the West. Hence few journalists are likely to entertain it."

Today, under banners of hatred and fanaticism hordes of the Islamic clergy command a veritable foreign legion of terrorists and their battle cry is "death to the West." They have unleashed a reign of terror from the streets of Tehran to nations all over the world including America with the bombing of the World Trade Center, Alas, there are still those who do not understand that terrorism is aggression and like all aggression must be forcefully resisted. Unless mounting warnings are heeded, the ayatollahs' war of terror will continue to surge unchecked all in the name of God. And wreckers alike former Attorney General Ramsey Clark who managed to attend the anti-American circus staged by the ayatollahs in 1980 will go on defending the cause of criminals including those who bombed the World Trade Center.

For my part, I never stopped denouncing the reign of terror in my country. When I finished this book in the mid-eighties few were those who believed me. Fortunately there is now a general awakening to the dangers and I truly hope that my writings will contribute to throw some light on the scouring of my beloved homeland.

Today, many of my compatriots at home and abroad remember with tears in their eyes my beloved brother Mohammad Reza Pahlavi, architect of modern Iran who died in bitter and exile.

Since he left us, war, destruction, torture, terror and countless executions have taken their heavy toll and left their dreadful mark on our society. Even those who helped bring about chaos have themselves been executed or fled the beleaguered country, victims of the monster they created. No doubt they too, will recall a sovereign whose sole purpose was to lead the country towards a great civilization, mindful that the essential ingredients of every genuine community are love, friendship, and mutual understanding. In keeping with the true teachings of Islam, he endeavored to elevate Iran to the ranks of the most progressive nations of our planet. He aimed to build its future according to the vision and the needs of a world about to enter the second millennium. Together with all progressive Iranians he was well on the way to achieve the goal that Iran would become the first of the world's ancient civilization to utilize fully the immense opportunities for material and moral advancement provided by the technological revolution of the past few decades.

"God willing," he said, "I should utilize the present opportunities to construct a modern and progressive Iran on sound and strong foundations, so that my presence should no longer affect the destiny of the country; for inevitably I will go sooner or later, while Iran and its society will remain. It is therefore my duty to try to insure within my lifetime that this society will become as prosperous and secure as possible."

Backward and evil forces did not let this dream come to fruition. Perhaps it is fit to recall that in his last message to his people, The Shahanshah cautioned that "hatred, vengeance, and massacre can never serve the cause of Islam whose sacred tenets teach us only justice, goodness, forgiveness and high morals ... Thus this explosion of hatred unleashed supposedly in the name of God is an insult to God and our religion. And this insult risks great wrong to Islam as the Inquisition once wronged Catholicism." "Our Great Civilization," he wrote "may appear to have died for all time. I believe, however, that like those powerful rivers that disappear underneath the mountains, lost to view, only to emerge later in full force, Persian culture will use to surface again, nourished by the values, thought, talent, and effort of the people. From their trial will be reborn both spiritual and material victories."

American author, John W. Limbert in his book "Iran at War with History" said that "even the most optimistic observer cannot help being discouraged about present day Iran: A culture denied; a people religious faith cynically manipulated and exploited thousands of young people dead, maimed, or in prison; an educational system in chaos and economy in near ruin and an educated population shouted down in a political arena that is given over to hate and the mindless chanting of slogans. It sometimes appears that the inmates have taken over the asylum and have tried to turn upside down the ancient Iranian traditions of creativity, compassion and tolerance."

So what is next for our tortured people and country following sixteen years of terror? Like countless of my compatriots look forward to a day when Iran will be free from the fear tyranny and terrorism. I do not get discouraged easily and as my late brother did, I too trust that Iran's rich cultural heritage, its traditional values, will rise to the surface again. It is my firm conviction that sooner or later the Islamic regime will disintegrate for the obscurantism it breeds lowers the level of intelligence to plain emotional reflexes. And all collapse of intelligence nurtures itself the germs of decrepitude. As said one of our scholar in exile "what is happening today with fundamentalism of all sorts, not only fails to renew the spirit of Islam, but instead transforms it into a funeral procession of petrified dreams vanishing in the sands of the desert."

The mullah's regime of terror and tyranny is on its way out. The past achievements of our nation throughout its long history, the resilience of our culture under the most adverse conditions, and Iran's almost unique regenerative abilities entitles us to such an aspiration and conclusion.

—*Ashraf Pahlavi*

APPENDIX

1. *Iran Times*, August 7, 1981.
2. Report number NS 165/76.
3. *Iran Times*, July 27, 1984.
4. "The Scourging of the Shah," a speech delivered by Russ Braley at St. Mary's College, Notre Dame University on March 14, 1980.
5. *Iran Times*, July 27, 1984.
6. *Le Monde*, February 22, 1982.
7. *The New York Times*, July 12, 1984.
8. *New York Post*, October 25, 1983.
9. Marvin Zonis, *Confronting the Shah With History*, Chicago, University of Chicago Press, 1980.
10. Number NS 165/76.
11. Number NS 232/76.
12. John D. Stempel, *Inside the Iranian Revolution*, Indiana University Press, 1981.
13. Cheryl Benard and Zalmay Khalilzad, *The Government of God—Iran's Islamic Republic*, New York, Columbia University Press, 1984.
14. Cited by Alpher, *The Washington Quarterly*, Autumn 1980.
15. Benard and Khalilzad, *The Government of God—'Iran's Islamic Republic'*, p. 206.

16. L'Express, February 3, 1979.
17. V.S. Naipaul, *Among the Believers, An Islamic Journey*, New York, Vintage Books, 1981.
18. *The Washington Quarterly*, Autumn 1980.
19. *Orbis*, A Journal of World Affairs, Summer 1979.
20. *Newsweek*, May 12, 1980.
21. *The Washington Post*, September 19, 1980.
22. Stempel, *Inside the Iranian Revolution*.
23. Richard Sale, "Carter and Iran: From Idealism to Disaster," *The Washington Quarterly*, Autumn 1980.
24. Sources for biographical material: Iranian Embassy reports, Iranian intelligence, books and articles by John Stempel, Richard Sale, Robert Dreyfuss, Michael Ledeen and William Lewis.
25. Richard Sale, *The Washington Quarterly*, Autumn 1980.
26. Stempel, *Inside the Iranian Revolution*.
27. Sir Anthony Parsons, *The Pride and the Fall*, London, Jonathan Cape, 1984.
28. Ibid.
29. *Orbis*, Summer 1979.
30. *The Baltimore Sun*, December 22, 1982.
31. Robert Dreyfuss, with Thierry LeMarc, *Hostage to Khomeini*, New York, The New Benjamin Franklin House, 1981.
32. Arthur Conte in Paris Match, March 2, 1979.
33. *Le Nouvel Economiste*, November 12, 1979.
34. *The New York Times*, May 2, 1978.
35. Jeanne J. Kirkpatrick, *Dictatorship and Double Standards: Rationalism and Reason in Politics*, New York, Simon & Schuster, 1982, p. 8.
36. *The Washington Quarterly*, Spring 1980.
37. Richard Sale, *The Washington Quarterly*, Autumn 1980.
38. Parsons, *The Pride and the Fall*.
39. *The Washington Quarterly*, Autumn 1980.
40. *The Washington Quarterly*, Spring 1980.
41. Ibrahim Yazdi, *The Last Moves in the Last Days*, Tehran, 1984.

42. Mohamed Heikal, *Iran: The Untold Story*, New York, Pantheon, 1981.
43. *The Boston Globe*, October 28, 1979.
44. Princesse Ashraf Pahlavi, *Jamais Résignée*, Paris, La Table Ronde, 1983.
45. Richard Sale, *The Washington Quarterly*, Autumn 1980.
46. Stempel, *Inside the Iranian Revolution*.
47. *The New York Times*, December 8, 1978.
48. Ayatollah Ruhollah Khomeini, *Islamic Government*, 1973.
49. Michael Ledeen and William Lewis, "Carter and the Fall of the Shah: The Inside Story," *The Washington Quarterly*, Spring 1980.
50. *Foreign Policy*, Spring 1979.
51. Ledeen and Lewis, *The Washington Quarterly*, Spring 1980.
52. Yazdi, *Last Moves in the Last Days*.
53. Parsons, *The Pride and the Fall*.
54. Cyrus R. Vance, Hard Choices: *Four Critical Years in Managing America's Policy*, New York, Simon & Schuster, 1983.
55. Sepehr Zabih, *Iran Since the Revolution*, Maryland, Johns Hopkins University Press, 1982.
56. Quoted by Zabih, from *Iran Post*, July 1, 1981.
57. Zabih, *Iran Since the Revolution*.
58. Robert Moss, "The Campaign to Destabilize the Shah."
59. Parsons, *The Pride and the Fall*.
60. *London Times*, March 16, 1980.
61. *Jeune Afrique*, February 28, 1979; *Le Point*, February 26, 1979; *Journal de Tehran*, February 19, 1979.
62. *The Atlanta Journal*, February 9, 1980.
63. *Penthouse*, August 1979.
64. Ibid.
65. *Le Monde*, January 31, 1979.
66. *Le Nouvel Observateur*, October 16, 1979.
67. *The New York Times*, January 1979.
68. *The Imam and His Islamic Revolution*, Victoria, Canada, 1982.
69. *Le Nouvel Observateur*, February 19, 1979.

70. *Newsweek*, January 29, 1979.
71. *Paris Match*, February 16, 1979.
72. *The New York Times*, October 7, 1979.
73. Ibid.
74. Cite passages.
75. See Law of the Talion in appendix.
76. *Le Monde*, September 22, 1981.
77. Source for estimates of political prisoners.
78. *La Clé des Mystères*, 1974.
79. *Sunday Times* (London).
80. Ibid.
81. *Newsfront International*, New York, August 1981.
82. Speech of February 6, 1979.
83. Speech of October 22, 1979.
84. "Fascism Without Swastikas," *Harper's*, July 1980.
85. *Christian Science Monitor*, March 5, 1982.
86. *Le Monde*, February 4, 1976.
87. *Le Monde*, September 22, 1980.
88. Iran Press Service, London, April 4, 1982.
89. *The New York Times*, February 27, 1984.
90. *The New York Times*, March 5, 1984.
91. Benard and Khalilzad, *The Government of God Iran's Islamic Republic*, p. 225.
92. *American Medical News*, August 7, 1981.
93. Benard and Khalilzad, *The Government of God Iran's Islamic Republic*, p. 165.
94. Reported by John Kifner, *The New York Times Magazine*, special issue.
95. *The New York Times*, November 18, 1979.
96. Reported by Terence Smith, *The New York Times* Magazine, special issue.
97. *Newsweek*, March 16, 1980.
98. *Washington Star*, March 25, 1980.
99. *Wall Street Journal*, April 1, 1980.
100. Quoted by Flora Lewis, *The New York Times*, January 4, 1983.

101. *The New York Times* Magazine special issue.
102. *The Sunday Times* (London), October 18, 1981.
103. *The New York Times*, January 17, 1983.
104. Number MDE 13/03/80.
105. Number MDE 13/09/82.
106. Number MDE 13/13/82.
107. Report for 1983.
108. Reported in *Iran Press Service* (London), July 1, 1982.
109. Letter addressed to the late Shah Mohammed Reza Pahlavi, dated April 25, 1978.
110. *Wall Street Journal*.
111. *Time* Magazine, August 30, 1982.
112. *The New York Times*, April 21, 1982.
113. *Newsweek*, March 8, 1982.
114. Summary records of the 47th meeting of the Third Committee, Document number A/C3/37/SR 47, November 23, 1982.
115. See *Canard Enchaine*, August 22, 1984.
116. Cited by Radio-Iran, September 2, 1984.
117. *The New York Times* Magazine, February 12, 1984.
118. Quoted by *Newsweek*, March 21, 1983.
119. *Washington Post*, May 10, 1983.
120. Op. Cit.
121. Reported in the *International Herald Tribune*, February 2, 1984.
122. In *Liberation*, April 15, 1983.
123. *Le Monde*, May 15-16, 1983.
124. Reuters.
125. January 25, 1985.
126. August 23, 1984.
127. *Le Monde*, January 29-30, 1984.
128. *Le Monde*, January 24-29, 1984.
129. *The New York Times*, April 14, 1985.
130. January 8, 1984.
131. January 11, 1984.
132. Quoted by *Jeune Afrique*, January 25, 1984.

133. Claire Sterling, *Terror Network: The Secret War of International Terrorism*, New York, Holt, Rinehart a Winston, 1981.
134. Ibid.
135. *Le Point*, February 2, 1981.
136. Ibid.
137. Joseph Rosenberger, *Death Merchant, No. 44*, New York, Pinnacle Books, 1981.
138. January 20, 1982.
139. Quoted by *Le Monde*, May 3, 1984.
140. *The New York Times* Magazine, December 16, 1979.
141. Reuters, December 21, 1983.
142. VSD, February 16, 1984.
143. Quoted by *Kayhan*, August 23, 1984.
144. *Kayhan*, September 6, 1984.
145. *Les Deux Directions de la Revolution Iranniene*, Paris, 1984.
146. Quoted by Bani-Sadr in his book, *L'Esperance Trahie*, Paris, 1983.

INDEX